WARNING:
According to the Culinary General
this cookbook may be hazardous
to your mental health.

JUANITA'S

eat it or wear it!

COOKBOOK

written by *Sally Hayton-Keeva*

Illustrations by Janis Kobe

Book Design by Nan Perrott

Published by Sagn Books

P. O. Box 216

Vineburg, CA 95487

ISBN: 0-9626295-6-1

Printed in the United State of America

September 1991

To my mother, Luvena Hayton, and my sister, Susan Hayton Magorien—both of them beautiful, smart and handy with a rolling pin.

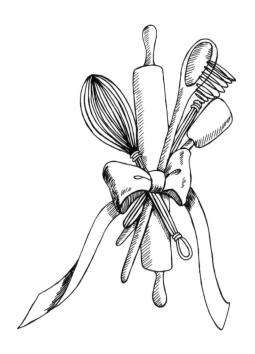

Other books by the author:

*Juanita! The Madcap Adventures
of a Legendary Restaurateur*

Valiant Women in War and Exile

America in Rebellion

The Mission

Index of Recipes

Soups: 11

Cort Mudge interview
Misbehavin' Chicken Soup
Actor's Special Split Pea
  ('Cause it's got lotsa ham in it!)
Great Depression Bean Soup
Clam Chowder Van Damme
Okie Vegetable Soup
Erma Bombeck's Favorite Corn Chowder

Salads and Dressings: 23

Frederick Mayer interview
Spud Special Salad
Polk Street Salad
Galley Green Bean Salad
Yank My Doodle (It's a Dandy!) Macaroni Salad
Carrot and Soused Raisin Salad
Kick-in-the-Kidney Salad
Ham It Up Salad
Pickled Whatever
Oui Oui Dressing
Tickled Pink Dressing
Feelin' Rich Roquefort
Juanita's Million Dollar Blue Cheese Dressing

Poultry: 71

Dr. Francine Bradley interview
Two Birds with One Stone Chicken
Methodist Roast Chicken
Sally Stanford's Two-Alarm Chicken
Chicken Sebastiani
Fairweather Chicken
    (Sometimes Sweet and Sometimes Sour)
Pickled Chicken Innards
Nameless Turkey with Sageless Stuffing

Casseroles: 85

Dr. Philip Rashid interview
Cathouse Lasagne
Eggplant Dinghies with Rice à la Rashid, D.D.S.
Beauty Shop Spaghetti
Naked Spaghetti (What to serve
    when someone's stolen all the food)
Marge's Enchiladdies
Cabbage Weenies
Bookkeeper's Special Fettucine
Hot Tamale Pie
Chili Rellenos O Lay
Burned Out, Down 'n Out, Four-Alarm Chili

NOTES TO THE READER

Juanita was once called "the drinking man's Julia Child." She fed her customers to the point where they had to be removed from her premises in wheelbarrows. She weighed over three hundred pounds and had the tongue of a lubricated longshoreman. She gave free run of the dining room to her pet pigs, deer, chickens, monkeys and ducks. All of these things and something more lifted her like a hot air balloon above the mundane world most of the rest of us inhabit: a world of checkbook balancing, calorie counting, cost trimming, and restaurants with all the unique charm of fifteen-dollar motel rooms. The "something more" was that she didn't just serve food, she fed people. She fed their bodies and spirits, equally, with lumberjack quantities of prime rib and rib-tickling humor. "Here!" she'd holler, sashaying into the dining room, dressed in what appeared to be a circus tent, and with a rooster perched on her shoulder, "I'll bet my cock's bigger'n anybody's in this whole damn room!"

And that sort of person easily fills a book, so I wrote one: *Juanita! The Madcap Adventures of a Legendary Restaurateur.*

"Eat it or wear it!" was Juanita's rallying cry. Sometimes it meant that you were to clean your plate of its three pounds of prime rib, and sometimes it meant you were about to exit her premises crowned with a slab of ham or with a hamburger stuffed down your pants. Juanita's motto, chalked up on the wall, read, "Food guaranteed but not the disposition of the cook." This was fair warning that you might be entering hostile territory, depending upon your behavior, your food order, or if you had decided to dine out on a night when Juanita had been hitting the vinegar bottle which she kept filled with Scotch.

If the situation escalated to the point where a robust voice with an Oklahoma accent caught you around the throat

1

like a vaudeville hook with "Eat it or wear it!" you were in trouble. No matter how fleet of foot, if your impatience had led you to leave before your order reached your table, Juanita would follow you full tilt out the door, through the parking lot and down the street, with a plate full of scrambled eggs, or whatever, poised in one hand for deadly-accurate delivery. You might have earned this decoration for an instantly-regretted order for something she did not wish to cook, or because you had loaded up your plate at her bountiful buffet with a heavy hand and then refused to finish it—but if you didn't immediately renounce flight and eat meekly the food put before you, your next stop would be the laundry.

This didn't always happen, of course. Juanita usually does what is least expected, which is no small part of her charm. She might come lumbering into the dining room with a huge roll of industrial aluminum foil, eager to send you on your way with two days' worth of leftovers wrapped in a made-on-the-spot aluminum chicken. It was always wise, when eating at Juanita's Galley, to observe a few simple rules:

1) While you could get away with coming in drag, hair curlers, three-day beard, and backless, frontless and see-through dresses, you had better never, ever, come smelling of patchouli perfume. Juanita could smell it from the parking lot. If you saw her marching toward you, eyes aflame and nostrils quivering, it was best to run.

2) While some jokester may have told you to order your eggs scrambled, you were wise to notice what utensil Juanita was holding when you placed your order, for while a spatula applied to the backside is unpleasant, a rolling pin to the noggin is worse. Some days she would scramble eggs; other days customers might hear her shout, "Scrambled? Does that asshole expect me to stand here and SCRAMBLE eggs?" Ordering your eggs fried was just so much

2

easier on everyone. (Of course we all have days like this, when we just don't want to look another little three-egg pan in the eye. Normally if we suffer frequently from this aversion we do not go into the restaurant business, but this is not the time or place to be reasonable.)

Hailing from Oklahoma (home, incidentally, of the International Brick and Rolling Pin Throwing contest) Juanita cut her eye teeth on such Great Depression favorites as lard on toast, plain boiled spaghetti, and bean soup. An "egg fried in water" was a great treat to be relished again while describing this culinary departure from the humdrum to her envious schoolmates, who had only had THEIR breakfast egg poached. By the time she opened her first restaurant, lard on toast had been left far behind, but her recipes were still simple. They were also better, somehow, than many fancier recipes, perhaps because she always insisted on the best ingredients: real butter and cream, fresh eggs and vegetables, the best meat and poultry. "You start with good stuff," she says, "and there isn't any way you're gonna end up with crap."

From her first restaurant in salubrious Sausalito to the heart of the Wine Country and points east—but not very far east since she travelled with saucepans and stoves and chickens and pigs, like a circus—she has opened the doors to twelve different incarnations of Juanita's Galley. Sometimes she moved because she was restless and sometimes she moved because her restaurant had burned down, but she always had a devoted band of customers who would follow her from town to town, county to county, to ever more improbable locations. No matter where she drove in her tent stakes, her food remained the same: good, heartland America fare with stick-to-the-ribs wholesomeness and honest flavor.

I have listened to at least a hundred fond reminiscences of—"that prime rib!" "That heavenly roast chicken!" "Oh, I can still taste her chili rellenos!"—all said almost in whispers, accompanied by pats on the belly and groans of overindulgence remembered. To eat at Juanita's Galley was to have Thanksgiving with the family any day of the year. "Eat! Eat! You're gonna starve to death!" thundered from on high, while a flood of enchiladas, flapjacks and black-eyed peas poured forth from the kitchen. To eat at Juanita's was to swear that you would never be able to eat anything ever again.

Pinning Juanita down for recipes has been a challenge for a sumo wrestler since she has always been too busy with the details of living to write most of them down at all. A few sheets survived, splattered with grease and dollops of dressing, but for the most part they survive in her memory. I followed her, notebook in hand, for weeks as she offered directions like, "Well, honey, hell! You just buy yourself a big wheel of real good imported blue cheese and thwack it on your counter and mush it up with your hands and then..." Cooking as Physical Therapy, perhaps?

I will never forget the discussion we had about fried and roasted chicken. It was similar to most of our culinary discussions and somewhat more lucid than many. It went like this:

Me: "Now, let's see, with the fried chicken, you rolled it in seasoned flour and then fried it in hot oil."

Juanita: "You forgot about washing."

Me: "Washing?"

Juanita: "In milk."

Me: "What?"

Juanita: "You want all your flour to fall off?"

Me: "No."

Juanita: "And bake it."

Me: "You bake your fried chicken?"

Juanita:	"No, you asshole, you bake your ROAST chicken."
Me:	"Well, then, what do you do with your fried chicken?"
Juanita:	"You don't."
Me:	"You don't what?"
Juanita:	(with a sigh) "You don't bake it."
Me:	"But I thought you just said you baked your fried chicken?"
Juanita:	"But then it wouldn't be fried, would it?"
Me:	"Uh, I guess not."
Juanita:	"Well, then, there ya go."
Me:	"So with your roast chicken, you wash it first in milk and then roll it in seasoned flour and then bake it."
Juanita:	"Only fry it awhile first and then bake it."
Me:	"The baked chicken?"
Juanita:	"No, the fried chicken."
Me:	"But if you do exactly the same thing with both chickens, they're both the same recipes."
Juanita:	"No they're not."
Me:	"But both are fried and both are baked."
Juanita:	"No, only the baked is baked. The fried is fried." (deep sigh) "Ya know, you're gettin' me real depressed. Why don't we hit a yard sale?"

I have condensed such "Who's on First" recipe recitals to what we finally ended up with after sliding head first into home plate.

Eventually the recipes were either dredged up from her really remarkable memory or gathered from her friends, who often added to her buffet with specialities of their own. Thus we have Micki Smircich's Dirt Cake and Dr. Philip Rashid's Cabbage Weenies and Marge Turnauer's Enchiladdies. These dishes added a cosmopolitan flair to many a dinner at Juanita's and are added, with gratitude from the author, to this culinary—and literary—smorgasbord. Please your family and delight your friends and remember, that while you can use margarine and lowfat sour cream and pseudo-salt, to truly savor the original dishes you must go wild in the grocery dairy case, throw caution to the winds and dig in.

Enjoying food as so very many of us do, I was not dreading the essential cookbook-related task of testing the recipes—once I'd gotten my hands on them. Dr. Philip Rashid met me one afternoon at Juanita's home to taste-test his delicious Eggplant Dinghies. Juanita turned out not to be there at the time, having committed herself to cleaning a friend's house in exchange for a large aquarium which now graced the front porch. It seemed to me an uneven exchange due to the probability that if the house were as dirty as the aquarium, Juanita, at that very moment, would be driving a forklift through her friend's living room. Goldfish were swimming uncertainly through the muck, nudging rocks, perhaps hoping to find the plug. I had brought some large snails, not to be eaten but to eat, and tossed them into the aquarium. One died instantly on impact; the second stayed toe-upward for the duration. Only the other two seemed at all inclined to pursue existence in their new, and darker, universe. Near the aquarium was Juanita's rabbit (who always bites her when she tries to pet him, much to her amusement) and a large cage for her pet rooster, Chickenshit IV, and his harem of Rhode Island Reds.

(Since Juanita has long been known for her kindness to abandoned animals—the more abandoned the better— her living quarters have always been more wildlife waystation than residence. Chickens have appeared on her doorstep at midnight, clutched by the foot by some unhappy owner. Cats with their kittens and ancient, hairless dogs regularly limp and snarl into Juanita's bed and heart. She has never been able to say no to anyone with a toothless scrap of fur in his arms. Heaven, to Juanita, is another mouth to feed.)

Dr. Rashid arrived bearing a casserole of Eggplant Dinghies, and was crestfallen at the news that Juanita was elsewhere. However, making the best of our opportunity, we gingerly stepped inside her house. The sound of the door opening sent a few of the more feral animals diving for cover under Juanita's bed, but there still remained a baker's dozen of cats resting on every horizontal surface like last week's helium balloons. We threaded our way through a low and bumpy wilderness of chairs, ceramic roosters, clothes mangles, palmetto fans, trunks, artificial flowers, dead potted plants and tottering piles of magazines and crockery, to two chairs, one of which bore a saucer of partly-petrified pork chop. I moved this feast farther back into no-man's-land and sat. Dr. Rashid, a short and very charming periodontist, perched on the other chair, clutching his casserole as if fearing that a cat might launch a first strike at the Eggplant Dinghies which were, after all, the *raison d'être* of our meeting.

We were warmly welcomed by Juanita's little dog, Chippie, while a cat on a windowsill hung peering upside-down over the doctor's left shoulder. For a moment overcome—even though we are both accustomed to Juanita's unique sense of interior decoration—we looked around us at the walls. A beautiful antique mirror bristled with photographs of other people's children, pictures of Jesus framed in seashells hung at either side of her open bedroom door, a large print of two cats dressed as Pilgrims and holding a large roast turkey on a platter adorned the far (if twelve feet can be described as "far") living room wall. Since there is no door to the kitchen we could see the electric woks and prehistoric microwave oven that are the only cooking appliances Juanita now owns—if you do not count the large and cracked barbecue smoker sitting in her yard near where some of her chickens live in an old Airstream trailer. (The effect, especially when the chickens are all out and the roosters are swept up in tribal warfare, is rather like a Saturday Night Live interpretation of *Animal Farm*.)

Equipped with paper plates and utensils excavated from Juanita's kitchen, we assayed the eggplant and found it delicious, even though I had the feeling that it might have tasted even better in other circumstances. Maybe not. Juanita's Galley kitchens, while always clean and occasionally organized, were often the rendezvous for her adopted animals. Dr. Rashid and I decided, mouths full of eggplant, that though the Galley had been somewhat less crowded, it still had resembled, in color and wildlife, the surroundings in which we were conducting the first of our taste-tests. We left the remainder of the casserole in Juanita's refrigerator because she loved Dr. Rashid's Eggplant Dinghies and would have been sorry—and perhaps made us sorry, too—if she had not been included in the feast.

The following week, with Cabbage Weenies on the agenda, Dr. Rashid and I arrived at Juanita's front door to find only the rabbit and surviving goldfish on sentry duty. Inside her living room the cats, Chippie and an assortment of fleeing shadows greeted us from the gloom. We stood uncertainly on the doorstep, Dr. Rashid clutching a cabbage and a package of sirloin to his chest. It was not an inviting interior, although it surely was an interesting one, so we backed out and went in search of the elusive Juanita, herself. The local postmaster gave us directions to the house she had been obsessively cleaning for nearly two weeks and soon we were being swept inside a spotless— and very empty—house by the legendary restaurateur. Dressed in several layers of muumuu, apron and jacket, she was surrounded by an industrious work crew of recent arrivals from South of the Border. Since she does not speak Spanish and they were not yet in command of English, it was a suburban Tower of Babel full of armwaving, curses and startled exclamations. Dr. Rashid and I gave up on the instant any lingering thought of Cabbage Weenies, and helped put up curtains. Juanita, as everyone who knows her knows, is a vortex into which all other realities are sucked, churned about and spat out again; a sometimes fearsome but usually exhilarating experience in which mind-altering drugs are entirely unnecessary.

Since enormous amounts of each dish in this book have been eaten, I have been content with sampling whatever I have felt like sampling, in an unscientific but perfectly enjoyable way. I made Pork Loins in Bed for my husband, who pronounced them good enough to eat often, especially with the Save Your Soul Sauerkraut which composes the bed. On several weekends we tried the Standing Room Only Lamb Shanks and the Desperation Bread Pudding, patting our pleasantly rounded bellies afterward with a gratifying sense of a job well done. Juanita made us the ribs and black-eyed peas on New Year's Day, the peas ensuring that we wouldn't get divorced or be hounded by a creditor all year. On Thanksgiving we ate her Nameless Roast Turkey and Sageless Stuffing, accompanied by all of the other dishes Juanita considers Minimum Daily Requirement for holiday feasts. We groaned gently and survived.

The problem has been—as the knowledgeable cook will soon notice—portion size. Juanita has always cooked for the multitudes, even when only two were expected to dinner. I, who dislike the term "portion" and get nervous around any combination of words that involves food and size, let Juanita make the decision about whether we should cut down recipes from "Serves Forty" to "Serves Four." Her answer was, "You can cut it down to family size if you want to go to all that damned trouble." It will be easier, she implies, if you just get a bigger family.

9

Relieved, I made my own adjustments, sometimes ending up with half-dressed beans and sometimes beans swimming in a sea of red wine vinegar. (I would have been brained with a rolling pin if I'd done that in HER kitchen.) Nonetheless, trial and error is an honorable method and I suggest that any reader wanting to assay one of the restaurant-sized recipes either invite a great many friends in or plan on eating Kick-in-the-Kidney Salad until Christmas.

At any rate, I hope you have as much fun as I had in cooking, as it were, in Juanita's kitchen. Cook up a storm, add and subtract, careen off the beaten track, and when your friends and family are gathered around, smacking their lips and begging for more, pile their plates as if you were Juanita herself, and holler, "Eat it or wear it!" They'll eventually get used to the New You and love you even more. Trust me.

Sally Hayton-Keeva, April 19, 1991.

Soups

"Misbehavin' Chicken Soup"

CORT MUDGE:

Juanita's Galley was the true Sausalito. There was the hill life and the street life, and though Juanita herself was a member of the street variety, her restaurant pulled in people from all walks of life. That's part of what made her place so interesting. Of course she proved that she could run her unique style of restaurant in a variety of places and succeed in all of them. I think this was because people took a proprietary interest in her restaurants and felt very involved and connected to them. She encouraged a real sense of community, even though she was often given to throwing food and slapping people around. I once saw her fling a plate loaded with breakfast at a departing car and then come right on back into the restaurant as if nothing had happened. Most of the people she threw food at understood this was just her way of communicating. Communicating by one-way food fight, maybe, but it got her point across, didn't it?

You could actually tell a lot about people by the way they related to Juanita. It was kind of a trial by fire. Almost everybody I took with me were crazy about the Galley. I always felt that Juanita was someone you wanted to share with somebody you loved—or thought about loving—and sharing an experience like Juanita was a way to get close fast since nobody could just sit there like a rutabaga when Juanita was around! She provoked a lot of honest conversation.

For awhile I ran a coffeehouse, but when I was forced to close it down I was pretty hard up financially. Juanita fed me one whole winter—on a long, long tab. I paid her back but I'm certain that if I hadn't, it wouldn't have mattered. She would've fed me just the same since her joy was in feeding people, not getting rich. I would go in for breakfast or dinner and often end up doing dishes for her. Other people were always willing to do things for her since it was fun and you just knew deep down that she would do the same thing for you if shoes were on other feet. When I would walk in the door she might holler, "Oh, Cort, good! I gotta toilet needs fixin'!"

I lost touch with her for awhile. I finally found out where she'd gone. It had been a long time, but when I walked in the door she yelled, "Oh, Cort, good! We need to get a drain put in!" That was her hello after so many months had gone by. I felt just like I'd come home.

MISBEHAVIN' CHICKEN SOUP

First off, I never put my own animals in anything I cooked. But I remember a coupla times I had a cock that bit me and so I took him on a little sightseein' trip of my kitchen where I had chicken soup on the stove. I just stood there and gave it a little stir or two and said, meaningful-like, "If you bite me again, you little s.o.b., you're gonna end up like HIM." It worked every time, never got bit again. I know this sounds like I'm makin' it up but it's the God's truth, honey.

For chicken soup what you do is, you take your chicken necks or whatever else is cheap and put 'em in a pot of water and bring it to a boil. Then you lower your heat and let it bubble away as long as you have patience for. Never never never put Monosodium Glutamate in it or in anything else. You put enough good stuff in and you don't need it and nobody ends up with a headache. You can put in your chicken feet if you have 'em because they add body to your stock. After the scum rises to the surface, what you do is, you skim it off with a ladle and give it to your pig, if you have one, or to the dogs. Cats aren't usually too fond of scum, in my experience. If I was in a good mood I'd throw in some of my beer sometimes, especially if Dick walked in and I had to hide the evidence fast.

Once you have your stock cooked down so it's gold-colored and fulla flavor, then you add your Vege-Sal* and your chopped up celery, though you better not add too much celery or your soup'll be too sweet. Carrots are the same way. Add onions, too. Never forget your onions because your onions aren't never gonna forget you, whooeee!

*Available in your health food store if they know what's good for 'em.

ACTOR'S SPECIAL SPLIT PEA
('Cause it's got lotsa ham in it!)

I always had a lotta ham around the Galley, one way or another. Some of it was two-legged ham and some of it was just plain ham, but there was always plenty of it on my tables. You could do just about anything with the kind of ham you eat and almost nothin' at all with the other kind, but that's neither here nor there. I served nice center cuts of ham, so we'd usually have scraps and bones left over from the steaks we cut up for breakfast. Sometimes we'd give this to somebody or other's dog and sometimes we'd use it to make somethin' else, like soup.

What I'd do is, I'd take any bones and boil the hell out of 'em. Then I'd strain the stock by lettin' it sit in the fridge overnight or I'd drag a rag full of ice through it. Then I'd put in my split peas and little chunks of leftover ham and let that cook a good long while over a slow fire so it wouldn't

14

get scorched and have to be thrown out in the garbage. I never did add onions to split pea soup. I'm not sure exactly why not but I guess I always thought ham was enough for anybody. The thing to remember is that ham can be pretty salty and so you have to taste your soup first before you add your Vege-Sal because your vegetarian customers can't eat the soup and if it's too salty your old people can't either or they're likely to keel over from blood pressure right into their soup bowl. Killin' customers is no way to get repeat business.

GREAT DEPRESSION BEAN SOUP

I used to make this soup all the time when I was a kid in Oklahoma. Five years old and I could make bean soup with my two hands tied behind me. Mother was workin' at Froug's Department Store and wouldn't get home until supper time, so my main chore of the day was to stay outta trouble and have somethin' on the table by the time Mother got off work and figured out where we were livin' that day. I used to move us pretty regular when I was a kid because every other place always looked better to me for some reason than where we were livin' at the time. Once I got us into this bee-yoo-tiful apartment because it had a piano in it and I always did like the look of a room with a piano in it. I didn't want to take piano lessons—honey, I didn't want to take lessons in ANYTHING 'cept mischief— it was just the look of the thing. Generally I'd let Mother know where she could find where I'd moved her things and my two shoeboxes fulla stuff, and she'd come staggerin' in the front door, dog-tired, and I'd serve her up bean soup pretty regular.

What I did is, I took my beans and soaked 'em overnight in water with a little pinch of bakin' soda in it. In the mornin' you pour the water out. This is the way you get the beans softened up but also you burp less after supper. We'd always use pinto beans. Remember never never never to salt your beans while they're cookin' or you'll end up with little rocks. That reminds me of the time I was supposed to be makin' bean soup only I was out playin' kickball in the street and didn't remember my soup until it was burnt. So I went off to the grocery and got another bag of pintos and put those on to cook, only I got all mesmerized by kickball again and forgot that batch like I had the first one and had to go on back to the grocery store for more beans. On THAT trip back I was runnin' because time was gettin' mighty low and I dropped the bag a' beans and they scattered ever' which way on the ground but I was so rushed that I just scraped them back into the bag, rocks and all, and ran home and threw 'em in the soup pot without thinkin' of gettin' the rocks out first. That night my poor mother bit down on one and almost broke her teeth. Actually she did sorta crack one a little so I figured it might be a good idea not to tell her what had happened. I'd learned by then that it wasn't always a good idea to tell the truth, except when people are gonna find out later. Mother found out when she paid the grocer's bill and I found out right soon after that.

After your beans have soaked you put in fresh water and some salt pork if you have it. If you have a soup bone, use that to add a little flavorin'. Add your Vege-Sal and some chopped up onions if you want to, but you'd be surprised how tasty plain pinto bean soup is. Gets tastier the hungrier and poorer you are.

After I started my restaurant I stopped puttin' anything in bean soup of an animal nature because my vegetarian customers wouldn't have much to eat otherwise. I'd put in butter, of course, to make up the difference.

Darrell Reed

CLAM CHOWDER VAN DAMME

Chowder and me go back a long ways, but the chowder I remember best is the one I made one night when I had the ferryboat. Some bikers decided to have a rumble without tellin' me about it. I stood there while jam jars and dishes were flyin' every which way, everywhere, and chairs smashin' through windows and tables knocked over. George was my off-duty deputy there that night and he was a real good fighter. He was tryin' to corral everybody but there were just too many assholes for him to handle. I was just absolutely livid, I tell you! I went into the kitchen and a bunch of 'em were wrasslin' around on the floor. Since I wasn't about to see my glass refrigerator get broke, I decided I had to do somethin'. Besides, it was George who was on the bottom of the pile and one of the bikers' chicks was beatin' the hell outta him. Well, I mean, I just couldn't stand by and let that happen, so I grabbed that gal by her hair. She was wearin' it in this big beehive hairdo and it was so fulla hairspray that my hand got stuck in it, like she was the tar baby or somethin'. After I pulled her up I remembered I had a big pot of clam chowder on the stove and I thought for a minute it might be a good idea to shove her head down into it, but then I thought, 'Hell, I'll just haveta make a whole 'nother batch,' so I just put my other hand 'round her throat and sorta choked off her wind a little bit. I encouraged her to leave the kitchen then, which she did pretty quick.

You chop yourself up some onions and celery and bacon and mess it around on the grill or in a skillet with some good hot butter in it. Don't brown 'em, just get 'em soft. Then throw that in a big enough pot and add water and cube your peeled potatoes and throw them in, too. Brown potatoes are just fine, you don't haveta get fancy with those red potatoes that are so expensive anyway and are just potatoes when all's said and done. When your potatoes are about done, then add your milk. You can add cream, too, if you're a high-priced cook. Plain whole milk is just as good, to my mind, but you have to add it hot. Reason I say this is once when I'd put two five-pound boxes of clams in my chowder, I poured in some canned cold tomatoes and the whole damn thing clabbered on me. The reason was I dumped 'em in cold instead of warmed up. I had to throw the whole friggin' mess in the bay. I never will know why I put those tomatoes in cold and I've never lived it down, I can tell you that! So let it be a lesson to you. Do as I say not as I do sometimes. Mostly I never made clam chowder with tomatoes, but somethin' got into me that day and I threw 'em in. This is about the time you add your clams, and don't be stingy about it, either. Clam chowder fulla potatoes is just potato soup and no amount of talkin' about it is gonna change that. Don't forget your Vege-Sal. Let people add their own pepper. They're prob'ly big enough.

Some people like their chowder thick and the way I thickened mine was to add flour mixed in butter or cornstarch in water. One trick you can do if you like to thicken things on a regular basis is, you mix up oil and flour in a big can or jar and mix it up good and then when you need some you can just pour it into your pot. For God's sake don't use olive oil unless you're real Italian and even then it isn't a good idea. It won't spoil any time too soon since the oil will go to the top, but then you have to mix it up good before you use it or what you'll get will be oil and clumps and your family'll go lookin' for a replacement. When your chowder is about done then throw in some chopped parsley and there you are!

Now I have to add just one story about fish stock. We used to go to all that trouble sometimes for our clam chowder and what you do is, you take your fish heads and boil 'em with the windows open and then you throw 'em to your chickens. One time I had two monkeys in the freezer waitin' for the taxidermist. They were real nice little marmosets I had livin' in coconut shells in my bedroom. What happened was, they were gonna have babies so I put 'em together in a cage and the husband ate the babies and then his wife died and then he upped and died, too, maybe 'cause he'd regretted what he'd done. The cook used to take 'em out to tease the new employees, tellin' them he was gonna put 'em in the stew that night. That same cook didn't like my wooly monkey, Beauregard, very much at all and so he'd take those monkeys out and poor Beau would go screamin' off like he was gonna be frozen, too. Once we had a big fish head in there, left over from a fish we'd eaten, and the cook'd show that to Beau, too, from time to time, as a sort of reminder. That was real mean, even though he was a pretty good cook otherwise.

OKIE VEGETABLE SOUP

There isn't any particular reason why this is called Okie Vegetable Soup, only I learned how to make it in Oklahoma is all. Carrots is carrots and I guess you'd eat the same thing if you were sittin' at a table in Montana or Massachusetts. Depends on who's cookin' it and if they put in the same things. Like, I never ever would put in turnips or parsnips in my vegetable soup, but other than that it was whatever looked good or was the season for. And if you like parsnips, put in parsnips, but just don't ask me to dinner.

We were livin' on Maybelle Street in Tulsa at the time. I had to stand on a chair to reach the stove, bein' short in all the wrong places. I'd get a big bone from the grocery and boil the hell out of it, until its marrow runs out, and then throw the bone to a dog. I never had a dog back then but I used to hang around with some. Skim off the scum and give that to the dog, too, unless you have chickens. Chickens will eat anything, even each other sometimes, so they aren't what you might call picky. Scum is probably dessert to chickens, like a nice piece a' pie.

Then I'd chop up carrots and throw those in first, and then throw in your chopped onions and potatoes and then everything else you got. Don't forget the onions, especially if you didn't start with a bone, because your stock will taste like tap water otherwise. Throw in your canned tomatoes and hominy, if you've a taste for it. I love hominy and I'll put it in almost anything, if I've a mind to. Hominy tastes like I'm at my Grandmother's house again and it's almost Christmas.

Last of all you put in your chopped cabbage and parsley because you don't wanna turn 'em to mush and you will if you jump the gun and put 'em in too early. Once I was makin' vegetable soup when I was little and I got so tired of the hot soup splashin' on my hands that I had the idea of puttin' the cabbage on a plate and then tiltin' it into the pot, nice and easy. Problem was, I dropped the plate into the pot and it sunk right down to the bottom and splashed soup all over the walls and counter and me, both. I had to wash the whole damn kitchen before Mother got home from work. Maybe you can come up with a better idea, but if you think you can throw in the cabbage from across the kitchen you might as well forget it. I tried it and it don't work, unless you were aimin' at havin' cabbage all over your floor.

ERMA BOMBECK'S FAVORITE CORN CHOWDER

That Erma Bombeck was a nice gal and she was just crazy about my corn chowder. She was so crazy about it that it got so's I'd have it on hand just in case she came in for some. I didn't do that for just anybody but she always seemed to perk up when she had a bowl of my chowder in 'er. It's hard to be funny on an empty stomach. Corn chowder is real easy to make, too, and fills ya up like bean soup only without the gas.

First I'd make a cream sauce by meltin' butter down in a pan and addin' flour to it bit by bit and stirrin' it like crazy. Let it get just a little teeny bit brown and not too thick. Chop yourself some onions and throw these in and stir 'em around, too. You can throw in chopped celery but you got sweet corn and on top a' of that if you add celery you're gonna end up with dessert. It's a lot safer just to leave the celery out and nobody'll miss it. Diced up potatoes is optional but it's like puttin' raisins in chocolate chip cookies. Nobody's fooled after the first bite and some people might think you're cheatin'. Then you add hot, but not hot hot, milk and stir that like crazy and then throw in whole kernel corn right outta the can, after you pour off the juice. Add your Vege-Sal to taste, and paprika if you're in the mood. Let your chowder just sit on a low fire until it's hot, but not hot hot, and keep it there, barely bubblin', until Erma comes in lookin' peaked.

Salads & Dressings

"Pickled Whatever"

FREDERICK MAYER:

When I first came to Sausalito in 1960 and opened a pharmacy, Juanita was one of my first customers. She'd pop in wearing one of her flowing muumuus, waving her arms and being the character she always was. There were a few great characters in Sausalito in those days but she was the best.

You could hear her coming a whole city block away. She'd be surrounded by a crowd of admirers and just shouting at the top of her voice. She'd make a grand entrance into the pharmacy and waltz right up to my cosmetic counter almost every day, especially in summer. She prided herself on not wearing any underwear and she'd throw her muumuu up over her head and spray herself with all different kinds of sample perfumes. The tourists would go crazy. They'd come running back to me, shocked, saying, "There's a naked woman up there!" and then they'd all leave. I'd hear her say to them, "Honey, if you ain't seen it before, you don't know what it is. If you've seen it before, you don't care." Just boom it out all over the store. Well, she was really hurting my tourist business so one day I had a talk with our local police chief, Sergeant Kelly, who was another character in Sausalito at that time. I told him that Juanita was scaring my customers away with her indecent exposure and couldn't he please do something to teach her a lesson and make her stop. We came up with a plan that as soon as I next heard her coming up the street I'd call him—he was only six doors down—and he'd show up to arrest her and take her to jail.

The day soon came. I heard her coming down the street, shouting, and I called Sergeant Kelly and said, "This is it! Here she comes!" So just as Juanita throws her muumuu up over her head and starts spraying perfume all over herself, Sergeant Kelly sneaks up to her, pulls his gun and shouts, "You're under arrest!" Juanita throws down her muumuu just as Kelly holsters his gun and pulls out the handcuffs, and she yells, "You little shit!" and grabs him by the scruff of his neck and the seat of his pants and carries him out of the pharmacy. Now Kelly was kind of small and Juanita was strong as a bull and she just hoisted him along outside like a sack of flour and tossed him into the gutter. After that I never fooled around with Juanita. I just let her do whatever it came into her mind to do. I was the laughingstock of the whole town. "I see you got Juanita!" people would say to me on the street, laughing, "I guess you gave her a real good lesson, huh?"

My wife and I became faithful Galley customers and as our kids were born we'd always bring them along, too. No matter where she'd be, the minute we'd walk into her place Juanita would yell, "Fred! You son of a bitch! You've knocked up your wife again!" In those early days my wife was always pregnant. Eventually we had four kids under the age of five and Juanita would be sure to remark on this every time we went to her place to eat, and at the top of her lungs. Of course we all loved her, just like everybody else. She'd play with the children and make them pancakes in the shape of animals. They weren't in the least afraid of her, either. To them, she was better than watching TV. She was funny, like a comedy, and the kids knew instinctively how good-hearted she was. She'd feed everybody. Nobody was a stranger. Generous to a fault, which was her biggest problem, really, because she'd give the clothes off her back to a complete stranger—and with nothing on underneath, too! She fed half the Haight-Ashbury druggies and straightened out more of them than you could ever imagine. Helped people with mental illness and those who were sick or broke. Fed them, clothed them—and threw food at them too, on occasion. She was wonderful.

One day we went there for lunch with an important guest. Juanita was carrying on as usual, cussing up a storm. "You son of a bitch! Here you are with your wife knocked-up again." I said, kind of desperately, "Juanita, I'd like you to meet my father-in-law, the rabbi." Juanita kept right on cussing until my words sunk in. Then she turned to my father-in-law and went on shouting about his no-good son-in-law knocking up his poor wife all the time and not coming into the Galley nearly often enough.

After that first time we always took my father-in-law along to Juanita's because he loved her so much for her goodness. We'd walk in and she'd always shout, "You son of a bitches! Where in the hell have you been?" One time Juanita was carrying on a spirited conversation with the rabbi. She had a monkey on her shoulder and, all of a sudden, the monkey cut loose and urinated all over her. She didn't pay any attention at all, it didn't faze her for one second. I tried to point out to her what the monkey had done, but she just ignored me, too, and stood there dripping, yakking on and on. Another time I was there with my father-in-law and Juanita came up behind me and slung her breasts over onto my shoulders—they were real BIG breasts, too—right in front of the good rabbi, who laughed until he cried.

As good as Juanita was with people, that's how bad she was with money. She'd call me in the middle of the night and ask me to come right over to the Galley because it had just been padlocked by the IRS for nonpayment of back taxes and she didn't have the money to pay them off. I'd go on over and give her what she needed to open up again. Once she needed $123 to pay a plumbing bill she'd let slide until they had cut off her water. Eventually the IRS did close down the ferryboat for good. Sally Stanford, who had once been a madam in San Francisco and was for awhile mayor of Sausalito, she gave a job to Juanita at her restaurant, the Valhalla, but that didn't work out at all. Both women were real headstrong and Juanita couldn't take direction from anybody else on earth. She was her own boss. Her own person. I wish she was back here in Sausalito. We need her to come back and shake us up all over again. There aren't too many real characters, real living legends, left in this world and we need all that we can get!

Darrell Reed

SPUD SPECIAL SALAD

I made good potato salad, if I do say so myself. I always cooked the potatoes with their jackets on and then let 'em cool and peeled the skins off, because if you peel them before they're cool they'll get gummy. Peel 'em with a spoon. When you have a bus tray full of 'em, then you run 'em through a ricer kind of trip or you can cut 'em into squares if you have to. I like a ricer better and they come out all the same size, like little worms. Throw a cup of sugar into your potatoes and let 'em set. That's the potato part and you can usually get somebody trained to get as far as this when you might have to take over.

Shred or chop up eight or ten onions, dependin'. I like to shred 'em, but suit yourself. Throw in a gallon of Best Foods mayonnaise. I always used Best Foods because some other mayonnaises are runny and some taste gamey as billy goats and you aren't never disappointed with Best Foods. I don't say this because I'm tryin' to get given a free jar, or anything, I've just always used certain kinds of stuff and that's that. Mix into your onions and mayonnaise one half gallon of sweet relish, only drain it first, and two large spoons of mustard and as much Vege-Sal as you want. I used to throw in chopped celery, but I quit the time two old ladies told me the celery wasn't chopped up enough and it bothered their plates. I decided then and there to put celery only into the macaroni salad so old ladies could at least sink their teeth into my potato salad and be sure of gettin' 'em back. Mix everything together and let it sit for at least 8 hours to get married. At the very last you add one and a half to two dozen hardboiled eggs. I always ran 'em through a ricer, unless I was mad at somebody and then I'd pinch 'em real hard. This serves about thirty people who like potato salad real well and about fifty picky old ladies.

POLK STREET SALAD

This is a two-for-one salad you can eat for dessert, too. I like all kindsa fruit myself and always had it on my buffet, sometimes cut up like this one and sometimes just a nice big bowl of plain fruit. I used to like to cut up a watermelon so it looked like a rabbit and dump the salad in that. My buffet was always elegant and told a story about somethin' or other. What you do for this salad is, you drain two cans of apple tidbits and one can of pineapple chunks and then throw 'em in a bowl with a bag of those teeny marshmallows and half a cup of shredded coconut, which I hate. Glue this together with mayonnaise and there you are. Shredded coconut reminds me of shredded carrots, or vice-versa, and I hate both of 'em. I wouldn't even give this recipe except other people like it.

You can count on this servin' about ten people unless they're all kids and then maybe it'll serve eight. Don't use the big marshmallows because somebody could choke to death on 'em.

GALLEY GREEN BEAN SALAD

This is just the kinda salad you can mix up in a jiffy for when your friends come over or if you're a church-goin' person and your church has potluck suppers. I guess this recipe serves about twenty and if you run out you can always use your oil and vinegar over again. Mix a gallon of salad oil—doesn't matter which kind, only I never use olive oil, myself, but you can if you want to—and a gallon of apple cider vinegar. Add your Vege-Sal and a cup of sugar and mix mix mix. Then you cut up enough onions to make a gallon and chop half a gallon worth of green peppers and throw 'em in the dressing. Open four or six cans of green beans and drain 'em well and throw 'em in, too. If you haven't been listenin' to me and you've used red wine vinegar you're gonna be sorry at this point because your beans'll turn a color nobody'll wanna eat. If you wanted to make brown bean salad you shoulda started with brown beans in the first place.

YANK MY DOODLE
(IT'S A DANDY!) SALAD

I made my macaroni salad pretty much like I made potato salad except I put celery in it. I didn't put celery in my potato salad because of loose dentures and I wouldn't put onions in my macaroni salad because of gas. I'm just that way with salads because some people can't eat one thing and other people can't eat another thing and first thing you know if you're not careful everybody's gonna starve or go eat somewhere else. Everybody knew what they were gettin' in MY salads, even blind people, because I always put things in the exact same place every time. I don't like surprises, especially surprises in food, and that's another reason I don't camouflage what I cook. Good macaroni salad is good macaroni salad and if you want to eat swamp lettuce then you better go someplace else.

One weekend my husband Dick was relievin' me at the Galley so I could go paint the town. He was makin' the macaroni salad and had it just about finished when he doused the bowl with what he thought was vinegar only it wasn't vinegar, it was Scotch. He yelled, "Who put the booze in the wine vinegar bottle?" and my friend Joe Foley said, "Need you ask?" I don't know how that macaroni turned out—maybe it was just whoop-de-do—but he threw the whole batch out and had to make fresh. Poor Dick, he couldn't hardly keep track a' me sometimes.

Cook, drain and cool half a box of macaroni. Run cold water over it or you'll have cement. Mix up a gallon of Best

Foods mayonnaise and half a gallon of sweet pickle relish, drained good, and a cup of sugar. Chop up your celery and mix that in and then add one and a half to two dozen chopped up hardboiled eggs. If you make this salad often it might be a good idea to get yourself some chickens. Nothin' like fresh eggs and they're pretty to look at too. This is enough salad for maybe twenty people, unless they're fishermen and then it'll feed ten.

CARROT AND
SOUSED RAISIN SALAD

I made carrot salad but I hated it, myself. I just absolutely, positively hate shredded carrots. Always reminds me of coconut for some reason. Once I was livin' in this foster home in an oilfield and the woman I was livin' with kept givin' me the same bowl of shredded carrots every damn day until finally I had to choke 'em down before they turned green on me. That damn woman hennaed her hair to a faretheewell and ever since I just simply cannot stand grated carrots or women with hennaed hair. My customers ate it, though, so I kept on makin' it.

Take a stainless steel bowl and fill it three-quarters full of shredded carrots and half a cup of sugar. Then you take a cup of raisins and soak 'em in hot water for a couple three minutes and drain them well well well. Mix this up with enough mayonnaise to make everything stick together. Some people add pineapple but I never do because carrot salad is not fruit salad and fruit salad is not carrot salad, thank God. You can serve about ten people who like carrot salad and if your bowl is big enough. A two gallon bowl should be plenty big.

KICK-IN-THE-KIDNEY SALAD

This always was a popular salad, maybe because it's fulla beans and most people like beans unless they have heartburn and then they'll generally eat it anyway and be sorry later. First what you do is, you take a gallon of salad oil and a gallon of red wine vinegar and a cup of sugar and some Vege-Sal and whip all this into a frenzy. Then you cut up half a gallon of green peppers and a gallon of onions and throw 'em in a bowl. Open three cans of kidney beans and drain 'em and wash 'em or they'll be slimy and to my mind there's nothin' much more disgustin' than slimy kidney beans. Dump the kidney beans in your bowl and add one can of undrained garbonzo beans. Pour your dressing over what ya got in the bowl and pull everything through it and let it sit as long as you want to but not too long, say about eight hours. You can use the dressin' twice and save the difference. I guess this serves about twenty people if it isn't all that they're eatin'.

HAM IT UP SALAD

We served about twenty hams for breakfast so we generally had some left over. I don't mean off people's plates, I mean left over in the kitchen. Sometimes we gave it to whatever dogs and cats we liked at the time, but generally we made hamloaf or pea soup or ham salad out of it. This was one of my better financial ideas, unless somebody had stolen the ham, which happened pretty regular. Can't keep track of every littlest damn thing. Ham salad is just ground up ham and with sweet pickle relish and mayonnaise added to it. Squeeze out your pickle juice real well so your ham salad won't be all runny because what you want to do is serve it on hot English muffins and eat somethin' outta this world. Save your pickle relish juice for somethin' like salad dressing or see if you can get the chickens to eat it. When you have animals around it's a sin to let your garbage disposal eat anything.

PICKLED WHATEVER

You can always just buy jars of this at the grocery but I always made my own. Now, rhubarb's another story. I always bought Ritz brand rhubarb—it's got a blue label— since it was the best, to my mind. Just open it, dump it in a bowl and there you are. Why cook when you can open a can? You can make pie out of it, too, but just plain rhubarb is real nice and brings up stuff from people about the good old days when everybody ate rhubarb except for the leaves. You eat rhubarb leaves and you might as well go lie down in a churchyard. Ritz horseradish is best, too. If you have a bad throat what you do is mix half and half horseradish and honey and let it dribble down your throat. Works like a charm. Other things on my buffet would be beets right outta the can with vinegar dressin' and celery stuffed with cream cheese or cottage cheese, dependin', and sliced up cheese and green onions and always lots of parsley around so everything looks nice and the ice don't melt as fast. One day some fool woman came in and ate all the parsley we'd decorated the salad bar with. Walked around it and ate the whole damn thing, just like a cow. Parsley fanatic is what she turned out to be. That's okay, everybody has to have somethin' a little funny about them or you have to worry. It's the guys that act like Boy Scouts every damn second who wind up shootin' people from overpasses.

Anyway, what you do is you cut up carrots and zucchini into chunks and pull apart your cauliflower and dump 'em in a pot of boilin' water with pickling spice in it. Boil it until you can almost fork your veggies and then drain 'em and put 'em in hot vinegar and oil you've mixed up and throw in some Vege-Sal. This'll keep in your fridge for a week but usually it'll be gone before then.

SALAD DRESSINGS

Oui Oui Dressing

Beat the hell outta one egg and then—and only then—add 3 quarts of salad oil and 1 quart of whatever vinegar you can afford. Wine vinegar is nice but apple cider vinegar is good for arthritis. Beat all this up and then add 5 tablespoons of salt, 3 tablespoons of sugar, 1 tablespoon of pepper and 2 tablespoons of paprika. This is all around good dressin', not as good as my blue cheese but it won't make ya fat, either.

Tickled Pink Dressing

This is good with crabs in a salad or shrimp. You mix up in your bowl half a can of chili sauce and juice from some pickle relish. You add this to two gallons of mayonnaise, juice from 6 lemons and one teaspoon Tabasco sauce. I guess you could add pickle relish, too, if ya wanted to, but I never did and never missed it, either. Better forget it.

Feelin' Rich Roquefort

Break up 5 pounds of Roquefort into small pieces and let 'em set out at room temperature for 2 hours. Then you add 2 gallons mayonnaise (always use Best Foods or stay outta MY kitchen) and mix well, then add 2 tubs of sour cream and a split of sauterne. If your pockets are lighter than usual you can always put in chablis instead of sauterne and that'll work almost as well but not quite.

JUANITA'S MILLION DOLLAR BLUE CHEESE DRESSING

My blue cheese dressing was the best ever. I'd use a whole wheel, six pounds, of the best imported Danish blue cheese, then I'd let it go room temperature and cuddle it all up through my fingers. Then I'd put in a gallon of Best Foods mayonnaise and squash that up into the blue cheese until the lumps are medium. Then I'd sprinkle Worcestershire Sauce over that and it turned a kind of light brown and then I'd stir in two 5-pound tubs of sour cream. After you mix all that together, you see what your consistency is, and if you want it thinner you put in some white wine and if you want it real thin you put in MORE white wine, and that's all there is to it. You can cut it down to family size if you want to go to all that trouble. I figured it out for Dick Musson once but he didn't even say thank you or kiss my ass. I used to have a millionaire in Texas send his private plane and pilot to pick up my blue cheese dressing and if Dick couldn't say thank you then to hell with him.

Eggs Done Eggsactly

"Here's Lookin' at You, Kid, Fried Eggs"

BILL BIHN:

I was born in the Egg Basket of the World and my Dad owned the largest chicken hatchery in the world at that time, in Petaluma. I took up where he left off until the hatchery business dried up and all I was left with was eggs. I moved over to El Verano, just north of Sonoma, and started an egg ranch there.

Juanita moved north from her ferryboat and started buying eggs from me since I was practically down the road. She'd come every week, wanting a hundred dozen eggs or so and sometimes more. She'd just dip into her blouse and pay me right there on the spot. She showed up the first time with this guy she was lovin' it up with at the time. She introduced me to him and then said, confidentially, "We're not going to get married because we don't want to spoil the romance." It fell apart later, though. Case of two-timing, it turned out.

After she really got rolling with her restaurant and needed more eggs, I'd deliver to her on a thirty day payment plan. I'd go every Monday morning to collect for the week's eggs and this one time I asked where Juanita was and just at that moment an employee came along with a huge muumuu on a hanger. He said, "Oh, Juanita's upstairs in the bathroom at the end of the hall. As long as you're going you might as well take this to her," and handed me the muumuu. When I walked down the hall, Juanita stuck her head out the door and I gave it to her and that was that. Later when I got home I told my wife, Margaret, and she said, "I really don't think you ought to do business there anymore if you have to meet her in her bathroom," even if all I was doin' was trying to collect my egg money. Another time I went to collect on my bill and was told that she was in her office down the hall. Turned out that her "office" was her bedroom and she was sittin' there in bed, wearing a nightgown and with her papers all spread out around her on top of the covers. That was her office desk, I guess. I went home and told Margaret about it, and she just shook her head and said, "I don't know about that Juanita." She thought I might be tempted, might be dragged into bed or something. Dragged right on into her office desk.

Most of the time when I went to collect on my bill there wasn't anybody there to pay me. I'd wander around and then have to go on home and Margaret would say, "That Juanita." It wasn't that Juanita ever disagreed with me about the amount of the bill, she always accepted what I told her and never argued the point. She had a hard time keepin' count of all those eggs, I guess, just like she seemed to have a little trouble keepin' count of anything. Had to do with her bein' on the wagon or not, so they say. I never saw her lit, myself, but when she fell off the wagon I guess she didn't keep too close a watch on things and stuff had a habit of disappearing out the kitchen door. Then, of course, a lot of food got thrown out and some got thrown at people, though I never saw that myself. She also helped out a lot of people who were down and out and lookin' for work or a meal. She'd take them in and feed 'em and give 'em a job. Good to people, she always was. One in a million, that way.

Actually, I never had any big problems collecting from her until her first place burned down and she moved to the big old hotel nearby. It was sort of a struggle for her to get on her feet and her account started backing up. At one point she asked me if I would loan her $800 so she could buy meat for the weekend and that she'd pay me $900 on Monday. Sounded okay, so I did. It worked out great that first weekend, but the second weekend I came up empty-handed and figured I was a partner by then. I put her on a cash-only basis and told her that when she had money she was to send somebody over to my farm for eggs and that's what she did from that time on. I think Margaret was kinda relieved, all things considered.

Juanita usually did well, though, even if she was sometimes low on cash. She ran a real different kind of place with a bunch of chickens and animals running around in her restaurant. She used to have this monkey, Beauregard, who would climb up on the buffet and help himself to whatever it was he wanted, though I never saw him head for my eggs. Some of the patrons thought that was funny and others didn't think too much of the idea. Didn't bother me one way or another. That monkey used to swing from a rope in the lobby and pee on customers, which Juanita thought was pretty hilarious. It took a long time for the Health Department to 86 the zoo, but things didn't get all that much quieter, considering Juanita was still around.

Darrell Reed

THE DEVIL MADE ME DO IT
STUFFED EGGS

Hardboiled eggs done right is what you have to start with, not anything else. Put your eggs in a pot of cold water. Don't do more'n about two dozen at one time or some'll be done and some'll be too done and then where'll ya be? Put half a cup of salt at least in your water so your shells will come off without pullin' half the damn egg along with it. If that happens you'll have to make yourself potato salad or you've just wasted time AND money. Bring your pot to a boil and then lower your fire to low and let your eggs just simmer for fifteen minutes. Take your pot off the stove and pour out the hot water without burnin' yourself (use Bag Balm) and pour cold water over your eggs to cool 'em down.

You can slice your eggs with a knife, but a serrated egg cutter makes 'em prettier for company. Take out your yolks and smash 'em good in a bowl and then add Best Foods Mayonnaise and Vege-Sal and dry mustard. Add whatever you feel like addin' since a little bit one way or another won't make much of a difference unless you're makin' 'em for your mother-in-law, in which case you can't please her whatever you do since she'll think her devilled eggs are better than yours anyway.

Once you got your yolks all mashed up, put 'em in an icing bag and squish 'em into your whites and then add just an itsy-size sprig of parsley to each one and then serve 'em on a mirror. You don't HAVE to serve 'em on a mirror but I did and everybody liked 'em that way so you might as well do it, too. Once this little fat guy came into my place and when Lee Rae went into the dining room, there he was, standin' at the buffet, slidin' the hardboiled eggs all over the mirror they were sittin' on and every once in awhile grubbin' one up and poppin' it in his mouth. We weren't even open for business yet, so Lee Rae, who'd made the eggs, decided to throw him out. Trouble was, he turned out to be the owner of the building we were in and we had to do some pretty fancy talkin' not to get thrown out, chickens an' all.

This may not happen to you, but once we got this couple in for dinner and since they had to wait awhile they were pretty well greased by the time they sat down to eat. She was this fatsy sorta woman with crimpy hair, the kind you know whines a lot about nothin', and she got up and went over to Lee Rae and took an English muffin off her tray. I told her to wait for a minute, for godsake, and the waitress would bring the muffins to her table. Well, she just started whinin' and lamentin' like I was starvin' her to death on purpose and so I decided to teach her a lesson in manners and threw a stuffed egg at 'er. My aim was always my pride and I hit her right in the kisser. Her husband had some sorta objection to this and yelled about how I'd be a lot nicer human bein' if I'd gotten myself laid and I said, "Honey, I'd love to, if I didn't have to stick around here and take care of a buncha assholes like YOU!" Most of the time I didn't throw the stuffed eggs because I had my rollin' pin or a skillet and didn't have to waste food. Don't stuff eggs you've dyed for Easter or somebody'll think somethin' weird's crapped on 'em or you've put somethin' funny in 'em. Unless it's your family and they have to expect eatin' eggs like that.

DRUNKEN EGG OMELETTE

Sometimes if I felt like it I made my omelettes with beer. This particular recipe got invented one day when I was drinkin' a beer and didn't feel much like goin' across the kitchen to the water faucet, so I just dumped the beer in and whoever it was got it liked it real well. After that I was real inclined in that direction, especially when Dick would walk in the kitchen—this was before my dry days—and I'd have to destroy the evidence. Drunken Pork Chops started up the same way. After I was supposed to be on the wagon, Dick would come into the kitchen and find half a beer and I'd say, "I just made an omelette," and sometimes he'd believe me and sometimes he wouldn't, dependin'. For awhile there I announced I could only make plain omelettes since Dick was lookin' at me peculiar.

Beat the hell outta your eggs and then pour in your beer and beat the hell out of 'em both. Melt butter in your slipperiest skillet and pour in your eggs. Pull at 'em a little at first and then let 'em just barely set. You can hurry things up by puttin' a lid on your skillet and that fluffs the omelette up even more than it is already. Once when I did that the lid practically bounced right off the pan. If you wanna add ham or cheese or somethin', you add that stuff when you put in your eggs. Don't fool around with puttin' it in last because that's just too finicky for anything.

NEST EGGS AND BAKED BACON

To tell you the truth, I never made eggs like this in my restaurant because they're fussier than scrambled, and scrambled eggs made me mad enough as it was. I'm tellin' you about 'em so you can make 'em if one day you wake up and want somethin' different. I got this recipe from this guy who was a troubleshooter in bakeries. He'd go around checkin' out whether or not they had the right kinda paint on their walls that didn't grow mold that'd fall off into the dough. He asked Dick and me over and over if we ever were in Vermont could we look 'im up. Dick wanted to shoot himself a deer so we went up to Vermont and stayed with this guy and next mornin' we woke up to broiled bacon and shirred eggs. The shirred eggs were good but the broiled bacon was a revelation, honey, 'cause I'd always done bacon on a grill. He made a believer outta me, though, and after that I'd bake it or broil it all the time. When you have a buffet you gotta do a lotta things fast and ya don't wanna burn too much stuff or you'll REALLY be far behind. So, anyway, what you do to make your shirred eggs is, you beat the hell outta your egg whites until they're puffy and then drop mounds of 'em into a pan you've greased good with butter. Make holes in the middle like they're nests and drop your yolks into the nests. Cook as long as you want. You can do shirred eggs in milk, too, but I never did think that was so much different than what we'd do in the Depression when we'd cook 'em in water. And if you can't figure out how to bake bacon, honey, you're in trouble.

ADDLED EGGS

My dear Dick often told me that it only takes five minutes more to do somethin' right, and whenever I hear that song "Five Minutes More," I think of him and wish I had five more minutes of HIM. To do scrambled eggs right takes awhile and is a pain in the ass. There was somethin' about scramblin' eggs that just downright addled me. Maybe it was all those dumb little three-egg pans. This guy who was the manager of a fancy San Francisco hotel and wore fancy clothes and had a fancy car and was just fancy in general, anyway, one mornin' he came in and ordered scrambled eggs. I told 'im, "I don't do scrambled eggs," but then I decided I'd scramble 'em anyway, what the hell. He sat there for awhile and then he decided, I guess, that since there wasn't much chance of 'im gettin' scrambled eggs, he might as well go somewheres else. Except by then I'd scrambled his eggs and didn't appreciate it much that he would leave after I'd gone against my own grain and cooked the damned things for 'im. So I took the plate out to his car and put it in his lap. Since the plate happened to be nice and hot he went "YOW!" and threw it on the floor of his fancy little sportscar. He wasn't too happy about it, but like I told 'im, I was only tryin' to help since I'd made him what he ordered, after all. Seems to me he didn't come back, but maybe he did when I was asleep.

What you do is, first you take your farm fresh eggs and crack 'em in a bowl and beat the hell out of 'em. Beat and beat and beat until they're all frothy. This is when you add your water or your milk and beat 'em some more. If you don't do it right you're gonna end up with white strings in your eggs and nobody likes that gunk first thing in the mornin'. Melt your butter in your skillet over a low fire and slide your eggs in easy and then pull at 'em and pull at 'em toward the center of the pan and keep on doin' that until they're soft and fluffy and cooked right through but not dried up. Never never never cook eggs over a high flame, 'cause you'll end up with a buncha tough eggs only your cat'll eat. Do it right and you'll have the best scrambled eggs ever, even if you hate to make 'em. Remember what I always say, "There's a right way, a wrong way, and Juanita's way." I learned that in the convent, right along with how to make sauerkraut and how not to lie, so you better do it my way and do it right. Okay, honey?

If you're scramblin' eggs for a crowd, crack two and a half dozen eggs into a blender and beat 'em up real good. When you think you've beat 'em enough, beat 'em some more. This is good for eggs and any number of people I know. Have a big enough pan sittin' on your stove with a half pound of butter meltin' in it, real slow. When your eggs are beaten up good and proper, pour into 'em one half gallon of milk and beat your eggs up again. Pour your eggs into the butter and wait until they start to set at the sides and then keep pullin' and pushin' at 'em until they're done. They'll be light and fluffy and the whey that comes out of 'em will keep 'em that way on your buffet, sorta like what you made is really a soufflé—not that I ever made somethin' as dumb as a soufflé.

OKIE EGGS

Okie eggs is great. If a whole buncha people came in orderin' scrambled eggs like sheep, then I'd just have to make myself a nice okie egg to get over it. Okie eggs are really mistakes on purpose since what you do is crack your egg in your melted butter and poke the yolk until it runs all over every which way and then fry it hard. Basted eggs were okay, I guess, but okie eggs got my dander back down after scrambled eggs had gotten it up. The other great thing about okie eggs is nobody can complain about them bein' done wrong since hard, honey, is HARD, no two ways about it.

FRIED EGGS IN WATER

When we were livin' in Tulsa, my mother and I, we moved one time to the Castle Hotel. I don't remember why it was we moved there, but I do remember that all the time we did live there all we had to eat was eggs one of her customers brought to her at work. I don't know if she gave us the eggs 'cause we lived in the Castle Hotel, or if the whole thing was just a coincidence, but we had lots and lotsa eggs. We didn't have nothin' to cook 'em in so we cooked 'em in water. You know how kids are in school, talkin' about how they'd had pancakes or somethin' especially nice that mornin' for breakfast? The first day we had those gift eggs, I remember sayin' proudly out at recess, "Well, WE had fried eggs in water!" All the kids were real interested and jealous since they'd never seen eggs cooked in water that way and thought it was a pretty fancy way of goin' about it.

Got to where I hated cookin' poached eggs almost as much as I hated scrambled eggs, because they're just so damned finicky to make! And you could just bet your boots that if some jerk ordered poached eggs, then you could be real sure that the next five jerks would order poached eggs, too! Sometimes I'd get so busy poachin' stupid eggs that when people would come in I'd tell 'em, "Fine, you order poached eggs, then you can set your own table!" And they'd do it, too.

This long-time mayor of Michigan used to come in the Galley real often and one time I caught one of my waitresses—we called her "Li'l Bits," 'cause if you didn't watch her she'd give everybody real small portions—well, she was tryin' to get that poor guy to eat poached eggs done the way he hadn't ordered 'em. I grabbed that gal by the nape of her neck and gave her such a shakin' she got whiplash and had to wear a neckbrace for weeks. I paid all her medical bills and she learned to cook eggs right.

HERE'S LOOKIN' AT YOU, KID, FRIED EGGS

There's any number of ways to fry eggs. First you gotta start with good, fresh eggs. I like the look of brown eggs but white tastes just as good, really. If your chicken's laid it that very mornin', then you got somethin' worth eatin' and it better be cooked right or your poor hen just went through all that misery for nothin'.

Put your skillet over a low fire and plunk in a good-sized lump of butter. Let it melt down real easy and then slip your eggs into it and let 'em set s-l-o-w-l-y. Nothin' I hate more than people tryin' to hurry eggs. I remember once Joan Sutherland, that singer, came into my Galley one day right in the middle of a fight I was havin' with my one-legged cook about how he was fryin' eggs too damn fast. I yelled at 'im, "I'm gonna rip that leg right off and beat you to death with it!" I guess Joan liked a little argument with her food because she told me it was the best breakfast she'd ever had. She came back real often after that, but she didn't sing. Ya know, some people just can't sit down and eat without some kinda fracas goin' on. Makes 'em feel right at home.

SAN QUENTIN EGGS

I used to hire these convicts from San Quentin and some of 'em were okay and some of 'em deserved to be in the slammer for what they did to my food sometimes. One Easter I got this murderer who was supposed to hardboil sixty dozen eggs for my egg hunt and when my back was turned he put all sixty dozen eggs in a big pot and boiled 'em until their yolks were purple. Well, I just took one look at what that asshole had done and whacked him upside the head and told 'im the next time he'd better get it friggin' right or I was gonna beat the hell out of 'im. He was a big guy but he knew a mad woman when he saw one and just kept his big mouth shut. I went off to the store and bought another sixty dozen damn eggs and when I got back he'd left, the chicken. Not only had he boiled 'em until they was practically petrified, he hadn't added enough salt and you couldn't get 'em outta their shells without a sledgehammer so we had to just throw 'em all in the bay. I would rather eat live snails than have eggs like that in MY potato salad! I heard later he went back to the guy in charge of the program and told 'im he'd rather sit on his ass in prison than work for me. Well, ha ha ha, if he'd had the nerve to come back to MY kitchen I'd have made him sorry he was ever born. Guess he knew that. So when you hardboil eggs, don't do it this way. Could get a man sent to the slammer.

Meats

"Pork Loins in Bed"

WARREN BACIOCCO:

Most of the time Juanita was in business she bought meat from my father, who was then the owner of the California Meat Company, as I am now. In those days I'd deliver her meat sometimes, myself, and then often stay to dinner. It was the best place to have prime rib and I know she bought the best because she bought it from us and it was all graded Choice. Just looking at her customers you could tell they were healthy meat-eaters by their exuberance and the good color in their cheeks. Not like those poor, pasty-faced vegetarians, I tell you! Each prime rib had seven ribs and she used to serve one and a half ribs with about two inches of meat for each person. This was the only place probably in the whole of California where you could get prime rib like that.

We'd usually go up there on a Friday night and deliver maybe twenty or thirty prime ribs and maybe twenty hams and it wouldn't be very long before Juanita would have run up a bill of twenty or thirty or even forty thousand dollars. We had a real hard time collecting from her, though. Her bookkeeping was terrible when she did it herself and she'd often spend all her money on stuff to decorate her restaurant rather than pay her bills. She'd forget, or something. Once when she owed us a lot of money she said to me, "Warren, would you rather collect or would you rather go upstairs and have me between the bedposts?" I told her my father wouldn't be too happy with that method of payment and that was that. It would often get to the point where we had to insist on being paid and she'd show up at our office in San Francisco, reach down into her bosom and pull out twenty or thirty thousand dollars and count it out right there on the counter. She could make change from there, too, dimes and nickels. Right in front of everybody, which was just part and parcel of who she was. Different.

Though she was always real cordial to me, she used to get in fights with her customers all the time. Once I arrived while she was busy throwing out a bike gang, hitting 'em over the head with a rolling pin in one hand and a baseball bat in the other. Holding her own, too. She weighed a lot and used her weight to advantage—but I also think she doesn't know what fear is and people sensed that about her. Sometimes a customer would complain about the service, because it was always real slow. Once one guy was giving her a hard time and she took the prime rib off his plate, stuffed it in his mouth, grabbed him by the collar and the seat of his pants, dragged him out of the restaurant and threw him down the stairs.

She went through incredible amounts of food and she was always urging people to eat more. But while it was all right for people to take home all of the food they wanted to, it wasn't okay with Juanita if their plate came back to the kitchen with food still on it. Juanita would ask the waitress where the plate had come from and she'd go out and find that customer and directly confront them about what was wrong with the food. She'd be real friendly but she'd put them on the spot. If they said the food was fine, she'd say, "Well then why aren't ya takin' it home?" If they said they didn't want to, she'd throw it at them. "Eat it or wear it, honey!" she'd say. A sweetheart sometimes and a real terror, too.

I always noticed that even when her place was packed to the rafters, if she saw an employee doing something that annoyed her, something that she could've taken care of with a whisper, she would scream at the top of her voice in front of everyone,

"You asshole! What are ya doin' that for!" It was a real floorshow but because of it I think a lot of her employees were only there because nobody else would hire them or they were real real broke. I know that they stole from her, maybe just to get back at her. There was a lot of pilferage. Once a fight broke out in her parking lot and while Juanita was trying to stop it, someone went into her kitchen and stole all of her meat out of the cooler so she had nothing to cook. Hams and prime ribs would go out the windows sometimes. Then on Monday Juanita would call my father and ask him for a verification of her order and whether it had all been delivered. Or she'd call me and say, "Hi, honey, how are ya? When are ya gonna come up and see me? And where's my friggin' meat?" I got very soon into the habit of taking careful count of everything and then counted everything again when I put the order into her cooler, just because I knew that by weekend's end she'd call and want to know what in the hell had happened to everything. This happened over and over again. Finally she installed locks on her coolers but they kept getting broken, as I remember. She just could never understand what was going on.

Other drivers of ours got along with her pretty well, unless they were real late and then she'd lay into 'em. Once one of our drivers put down her order too close to the cooler so that she couldn't open the doors and she got so mad she chased him out the door and into his truck, throwing steaks. And sometimes she'd have the delivery truck unloaded while she distracted the driver by offering him a cup of coffee or something. Then she'd tell him she didn't have any money for the C.O.D. and he'd drive away, not knowing he'd been hoodwinked until his next stop. Juanita was one-of-a-kind, but maybe the world can't handle more than one at a time.

BAKED HEAD OF HAM

First you have to buy yourself a good good ham. I like Victor's but there're all sorts of good hams in this world. Don't ever buy that godforsaken minced, pressed, gristly ham that's always on sale. It's on sale for a reason and that reason probably is that the ham tastes lousy and probably has pig noses in it. Pig noses and pig teats and pig belly buttons. You want yourself a good ham and if it's more expensive then you just haveta skip the next garage sale. That was always the hardest part of the restaurant business, since sometimes I discovered too late that I'd spent all my meat money on antiques or dirt. Then I'd have to scrounge and borrow and otherwise find some way of scrapin' together money so customers wouldn't haveta limit themselves to eatin' sauerkraut. A couple times I got someone to unload the meat van while I was gettin' the driver to look the other way, and that worked okay the first couple times, but after that they were on to me and I had to think of somethin' else.

Once I got my hands on a ham I'd cook it at 325 degrees for let's say eleven or so minutes a pound and then slice it all up and then put it back together so it'd look like a pig's head. I'd stick an apple in its "mouth" and maraschino cherries in its "eyes." Doesn't look much like a roast pig, but then you don't have to go to all that damned trouble. Once people start hackin' away at it it's not gonna look like much of anythin', anyhow.

ADAM'S DOWNFALL
BARBECUE RIBS

Men just can't seem to stay away from good ribs, and I always had some of the best, honey. I always used prime rib bones with enough meat on 'em to be interestin' because men like meat on their bones and I know what I'm talkin' about. This is a real good sauce for pork chops or chicken, too, but it's made for ribs like tit for tat.

Take a gallon of chopped up onions and throw 'em in your pan. Add half a gallon of chopped celery and one dozen chopped peppers, everything sauteed in butter until they're soft. Then you throw in two #10 cans of tomato sauce and three #10 cans of fruit juice that you've drained from the cans. Save the fruit for your fruit salad or use plain pineapple juice if fruit salad isn't on your menu. Bring all this to a boil and then let it just simmer by itself for maybe three hours. Vege-Sal your ribs and broil 'em in your oven until they're brown but not all dried out and dunk 'em in the sauce, or you can just as easily dunk 'em first and bake 'em later. If you want more zip then dash in some Tabasco or hot pepper flakes but better not do this unless you know the people you're feedin' like hot stuff.

STANDING ROOM ONLY
LAMB SHANKS

You take your onions and carrots and celery and tomatoes all chopped up in sorta small pieces and put 'em in a big pan. Then you take your lamb shanks and cuddle 'em into the sauce and sprinkle the top with Vege-Sal and put it in a medium oven until the meat's threatenin' to part ways with the bones. I always used Australian lamb shanks and at a dollar a pound, which was nothin' to be sneezed at at the time. People used to come to one of my places that was so damn small a lotta customers would have to stand outside on the street or sit on the back steps, lookin' at the garbage cans. On lamb shank night I'd just hand 'em out the door to everybody standin' there waitin' to get in. And if some customers got sick of waitin' and decided to go on somewhere else, they wouldn't have to go there on an empty stomach. I used to make over a hundred lamb shanks a night and that small place only seated about thirty people so you can guess how many shanks walked away. Just as well the Baptist church gave me such a hell of a time since I couldn't stay in that dinky place, anyway.

JUANITA'S WORLD FAMOUS PRIME RIB

There just isn't anything in this world as good as prime rib, if it's done right. Mine was done righty right. I had people drive for miles and miles to eat my meat and so I always felt I had to give 'em enough to satisfy 'em. That's the reason I always served a rib and a half, about two and some pounds, each. This way they could eat until their eyes boggled and not have to stop because they'd run out. If they had any left they'd always take it home to have for sandwiches next day or dinner next night. I never served child's portions of anythin' because I figured a kid should get treated just as good as a grown-up, and most likely better. No reason to starve 'em just 'cause they're short.

First of all you haveta get yourself a good prime rib. I never used anything but. One day this fool woman came into my place sellin' pre-cooked, pre-sliced, prob'ly pre-ate prime rib in plastic baggies and I said, "That shit you're sellin' will be sold in my restaurant only over my dead body. Now, honey, if ya know what's good for ya, you'll take a hike!" Crap like that's no better'n dog food. Matter of fact, I had a black poodle once that would only eat my prime rib and nothin' else whatsoever. Poodles are smart. But sometimes people are two sandwiches short of a picnic, boy. I remember this one time a guy complained that his meat had a bone in it. Can you imagine? I said, "Well, how in the hell do you think the cow stood up?" Lord have mercy.

I never roasted anything smaller than a seven rib roast. First you cut off the fat on top and rub the roast all over good with Vege-Sal. Then you tie the fat back on and slip celery ribs and onion slices under the strings to flavor the meat and the juices, both. Everybody always tells you to put a prime rib in the oven at 400 degrees and then turn it down, but I always put mine in at 350 and kept it there for three hours. Now remember that this is for a seven rib roast and I don't know how long you'd cook somethin' smaller since I never did. When you cook your prime rib this way you got well done on your ends and medium partway through and rare in the middle. So everybody's happy. Scoop up the juices and mash yourself some potatoes and maybe some creamed onions or peas and have at it. Girls, you'd be surprised to see how sweet a man can be once he's got prime rib in 'im, and when you add potatoes you got yourself a guy that'll show you a real good time.

PORK LOINS IN BED

This pork loin roast is Dr. Rashid's idea and just thinkin' about it makes my mouth water, it's that good. What he used to do is, he'd stab the meat with a skewer and then stick in slivers of garlic, the more the better especially if you feel a cold comin' on. Roll the meat around in seasoned flour and then brown it good in hot oil in a skillet. Then you turn the heat down and let it sort of bubble in there for awhile in a nice heavy iron pot for maybe three hours or more if you happen to forget it while you're doin' somethin' else. You have to put it in bone down, though, and fat up. When you look in the pot and it's nice and brown and gettin' soft, then you cuddle sauerkraut all around it and dribble a little brown sugar on top of that. Then you take a good sour apple and cut it up and shove it down into the sauerkraut. If more people show up hungry or you're havin' Irish people in to dinner, then shove some halved potatoes down into the sauerkraut, too. A meal in a pot and not much washing up afterwards, either.

BLACK EYE STEAK

When I started out I cooked everything in lard. I had this aunt that taught me how to cook Okie-style, with everything swimmin' in a sea of fat. Those were the days before they invented cholesterol and we all thought fat was dandy. Didn't know it could plug ya up like a weenie. The first meal I cooked for my husband Dick was chicken-fried steak. I'd saved up all my and my mother's ration coupons for the meat. Poor Dick took one look at it and told me that I'd better stop cookin' that way or I was gonna kill 'im and since I liked him too well to see 'im dead, I learned. What you do is, first you buy the kinda steak that's a rib eye or a filet, never the kinda steak that needs to cook a long time before you can get your teeth into it. You put your Vege-Sal in your skillet and let it turn brown before ya throw in the steak. When it's time, you turn it over to the second side and you never never never turn it over more'n once or they'll be hell to pay because you've spent a lotta money on the meat and you're just turnin' it to shoe leather if you turn it more'n once. The juices get seared right this way. Don't ever let anybody push down on your steak 'cause that squashes out the juices and you'll have to whack the cook good to get 'im to stop.

Another thing is, if you've almost mortgaged the farm to buy good steak, for God's sake don't fry it 'til it's dead. Rare is the way it oughta be, or medium if you have to, but never never never fry it well done 'cause then you might as well be eatin' jerky. I had to educate customers every once in awhile about how to order steaks done right and if they got stubborn and said, "No, I want mine well done," then I'd say, "Okay, asshole, it's your funeral." One time this couple ordered their steaks well done and then, when they got 'em, they had the nerve to complain to a waitress. Well, she told me what they'd said so I grabbed up my butcher knife and went over to their table, yellin' about how they could just get their asses outta my place, and

60

they started runnin'. Chased 'em right through the parkin' lot. Last I saw of 'em they were headin' down the street just as fast as they could go. Whoooeee, that was fun!

Another time this customer came in and ordered steak and he sent it back. We did it again and he sent it back again, only he was givin' my waitress a hard time and was yellin' at her. Well, I'm the ONLY person who could yell at my help and so I went runnin' out into the dinin' room and said, "Look, you son of a bitch, you can eat it or you can wear it outta here, take your pick." That hushed him up and he just sat there and ate his steak like a lamb. But once I got back in the kitchen, I remembered what that judge had told me once about sayin' things to people about their family, so I went back into the dinin' room and hollered, "I'm not supposed to call you a son of a bitch, so I'm callin' you an asshole." See, the judge explained to me that somebody can prove he's not a son of a bitch, but it takes a sight more provin' to show he's not an asshole. Words to the wise, honey.

DRUNKEN PORK CHOPS

I discovered this by accident, kind of. Durin' my drinkin' days when I didn't feel much like cookin', sometimes when I was makin' pork chops I'd just pour beer on 'em. I did that with eggs, too, sometimes. Still do, even though my drinkin' days are over. What you do is, you put Vege-Sal in your skillet and let it get brown. Then you put on your pork chops and however thick they are, that's how long you cook 'em. Only turn 'em over once so you have to get it right the first time. The minute you turn your chops over, pour in your skillet whatever you have left of a bottle of beer—you can pour in the whole thing if you're on the wagon—and let it cook down until it's almost gone and use the rest for your sauce. This tastes dee-licious all by itself and nothin' else added except for your potatoes.

Before I got off booze for good, Dick used to come in the kitchen and look at me real suspicious if a bottle a' beer was sittin' on the counter. So I'd always say, "This is cookin' beer, honey, not drinkin' beer," and I'd pour it over somethin' or another. This is the way I found out how accommodatin' beer is. I mean, just try pourin' Scotch in your eggs.

PUCKERED PORK CHOPS WITH JONATHAN WINTER'S CRAZY RAISIN SAUCE

Jonathan used to love to eat at my place. He'd put on a comedy act while waitin' for his flapjacks. Sometimes he had to wait a long long time because our cooks would be laughin' themselves silly and weren't stickin' to business. I'd haveta go slap 'em around a little if I wasn't laughin' too hard myself. I just love that guy and he just loved my cookin', so that's why he's got my raisin sauce with his name on it. You mix up half a gallon of any good fruit juice and add a box of brown sugar to it and two cups of raisins. Set your pan on a low fire and then what you'll do is, add half a cup of cornstarch that's been mixed in cold water and add it s-l-o-w-l-y. Let it simmer awhile before you thicken it and let it sit there awhile afterwards. You can put this on ham or chicken, but what I liked to put it on was pork chops. Sprinkle your Vege-Sal in a skillet or on your grill, throw on your pork chops, and when they're brown on one side, turn 'em over. I can't tell ya how long to cook 'em because I don't know how thick they'll be, so you're on your own. When they're about done, squeeze on some lemon juice. This perks up the flavor and kinda tenderizes 'em without addin' any of that fake crap that gives me a headache.

EAT 'EM OR WEAR 'EM BURGERS

Burgers and me go back a long long way and I'm real particular about 'em. When I started out in the restaurant business I just cooked breakfast for the fishermen. That was okay at first but then they started comin' back hungry after their fishin' trip but they didn't want ham and eggs again. So I started cookin' hamburgers, only I didn't know how to do more'n two at a time. These guys had to get home before their fish got rotten on 'em but I couldn't go any faster than two by two by two by two. Then one day this little fat guy shows up and orders ten hamburgers. I tell 'im all I can do is two at one time and he says, "Well, young lady, I'm gonna show you how to do ten at once." So I said, "Okey, dokey." Turns out he was the Chef Cardini that invented the caesar salad. He showed me how to turn the patties and get the buns goin' just right and when he finished his ten burgers he handed me money but I didn't want to take it so I threw it at 'im and he went away. We were friends ever after that.

Even though I could make ten burgers at once, thanks to Cardini, that sweetheart, sometimes people thought I was still too slow and would leave before their burgers were served. Well, I was tryin' to do my best and I didn't appreciate bein' left with a buncha friggin' burgers on the grill. One time these four cops came in for lunch and ordered hamburgers. I had bacon on the grill at the time, so I waited until that was done and then I cleaned the grill and salted it and put the patties on. I wasn't about to have those nice patties taste like bacon fat but those cops didn't even think about that, got tired of waitin' and left. Boy, did I see red! I grabbed up those burgers and slopped 'em good with catsup and ran out to one of the cop cars and threw the burgers in the window, yellin', "Here, ya gotta eat!" I mean, cops have to have their strength to deal with people like me. When I went back in, this criminal attorney was sittin' there and he'd seen what I'd done and he said,

"Do you have an attorney?" and I said, "No." And he said, "Well, it looks like you're gonna need one, so I'll be it from now on." He was a great attorney and did his best, but when he represented me I lost all five times. Said I'd ruined his reputation. I can't help it if I was guilty.

Get yourself some good ground chuck, and none of that real lean kind either, unless you're all plugged up with cholesterol and have to eat the kinda crap they feed you in hospitals. Make a nice round ball of meat and put it between two plates and smash it down, makin' damn sure you leave your patty about an inch thick. I had this one cook once who squished the patties so flat I finally had to say to 'er, "If you do that just one more time I'm gonna slap you in the face with it." So she smashes another one even flatter, just to get my goat, and so I picked it up and squashed it in her face. Then she started tryin' to hit me, but she was such a little gal that all I had to do was put my hand on her forehead while she just flailed away. Didn't land a blow even though I was big as a barn at the time. A cop came in to eat and said to her, "Joyce, take off your apron and go on home," so she did. She threw her apron the wrong way, too, and so I said, "You are never in this world comin' back to work for me," and she didn't. There was a right way and a wrong way to throw an apron at me when you were quittin' and she threw it in the air, not all balled up, so that was that. We stayed friends through the years, though, 'cause she was a nice little gal in spite of her cookin' behavior.

Clean off your grill and Vege-Sal it good and let it get browny. Sear your meat on one side and then flip it over to a new spot, not on top of your old spot where your Vege-Sal is gone. You can tell when a hamburger patty is rare because when you poke it with your finger it gives some and when it's real done it don't. If you want it medium then it's halfway between the two and you have to figure out that for yourself. Once I had these two cooks that would try to hurry up the patties by smashin' 'em down on the grill when I wasn't lookin'. Well, that just squashes the juice outta the meat and riles me no end. I'd hear this ssshhhh noise and turn around and there they'd be squishin' burgers. I warned 'em once not to do it again but I no more'n had my back turned when they started that damned squishin' again and so I fired 'em. I grabbed their spatulas right outta their hands and swept all the burgers off the grill. Towin' those two assholes behind me, I marched into my dinin' room and said to all the people, "These dickheads were ruinin' your food and so I've fired 'em. Now, if you wanna wait until I can catch up on all your orders, great, but if you want your money back, just go to the cashier and she'll give it to ya. And if you have any dogs or cats you can take the squished burgers home." Nobody moved except to raise their hands for the doggie bags, even though some of 'em had been drinkin' coffee until their eyes were buggin' outta their heads. Those people waited up to three hours for their lunch! I guess whenever I had a spatula or a rollin' pin in my hand, people just generally did whatever it was I wanted 'em to. And don't forget, I made the best burgers in the world and the best of anything needs a little more time, includin' you-know-what.

Now, you could preference a bun or an English muffin, and I always buttered 'em and toasted 'em on the grill. That and the good meat were the secrets of my success. 'Course, we'd always put on tomatoes and lettuce and all that rabbit stuff, whatever people wanted or whatever I felt like doin'. Some days I felt fancy and some days I felt more like sayin', "Oh, go cook it yourself," and then goin' to sleep.

MOTHER'S MEATLOAF

My mother let me go in the kitchen and get burnt on the stove just so long as I didn't catch myself on fire. Likewise, if I was good, she'd let me use her sewin' machine, which I just loved to play with. Cookin' was somethin' I HAD to do because Mother had to work so hard down at Froug's Department Store all day. When I'd act up she'd tell me she was gonna trade me for one of the nicer little girls that came into the store and I'd get real mad and tell her, "Well, of course they're actin' nice, they're gettin' a new dress!" Most of the time Mother and I got along just great, but I was really and truly a handful a lotta the time. Mother taught me how to make bean soup and meatloaf by the time I was six years old. Meatloaf was for special because it was the Depression and we couldn't afford meat too often. Maybe that's why in my restaurants I used to serve people more meat than they could eat, just because I remember not havin' much of it when I was young.

Anyway, what you do is, you take a pound and a half of hamburger and mash it up with half a pound of pork, ground up. Your hands work real well for this and it's fun squishin' the meat through your fingers. Chop yourself up an onion and a green pepper and squish that into the meat, then add two beaten eggs and maybe half a cup of breadcrumbs and mush everything all together. Make yourself a little loaf and put it in a pan and then pour a can of tomatoes over it and cook it for an hour and a half, maybe, at 350 degrees. It's good to know on this recipe how long it takes to cook, since people will wait a long time for some dishes but there just isn't too many people nowadays who will wait around for meatloaf. That's a sad fact, but there you are.

Some days when I made meatloaf in my restaurant I left out the pork part because there didn't seem to be much point in it. You can make it whichever way you want, but just don't put on tomato sauce because tomatoes is better. You haveta use tomato sauce in spaghetti so you got enough sauce to go around, but other times tomatoes is the way you wanna go. Pepper it after, always. It just gets my goat when people salt and pepper, salt and pepper the hell outta everything before it even has a chance to get itself cooked.

PEPPERY BEEF

This is fast an' easy and cheaper than a Chinese restaurant to fix at home when your family starts whinin' "Meatloaf AGAIN?" 'Course they're lucky to have more'n bald spaghetti on the table but there's no earthly use your tryin' to tell 'em that since they'll just look at ya like they know what you're next gonna talk about is walkin' forty miles through the snow to school wearin' nothin' but tree bark.

Pile up on your counter some good steak, but not too good, and some onions and bell peppers. Cut your onions into fourths and slice up the peppers and the beef in strips. Get your skillet smokin' hot with butter and throw in your veggies and stir 'em around until they go limp on ya and then throw in your meat and stir the whole mess. Pour in some soy sauce and dump it all on steamed rice. I can't tell ya how many people this'll serve since I don't have the least idea how much you're makin' in the first place. A good way to know if you've got enough for everyone is to look at it when it's piled up on your counter and if it looks like enough it probably is. You can always make more rice. You can also add garlic if you're feelin' a cold comin' on but I generally didn't do that in my restaurants 'cause some people are romantic and think that garlic might get in the way of their love life. I always thought that a man who can't handle the smell of garlic probably can't handle me, either, but then I've always liked my men laid back, if you know what I mean.

DISAPPOINTED DOG HAMLOAF

Leftover ham is a good thing to have in the kitchen since you can do so many things with it and if you get sick of lookin' at it you can always give it to someone's dog. Before I figured out how to make hamloaf, I used to give away boxes and boxes of ham scraps, and sometimes I still did when I didn't feel like fussin' with makin' a hamloaf. Dogs is real partial to ham and some dogs would come from a long way off to get themselves a nice slice 'a ham. Sometimes they'd just be outta luck, though. Business is business.

Take all your scraps of ham and grind 'em up and mix in a coupla beat up eggs and enough breadcrumbs to make it stick together and not fall to pieces. Mush it up good with your hands and smack it into a loaf and put it in a pan and bake it at 325 degrees until it's done. I can't tell you how long unless I know how big your loaf is. If you're makin' a great big hamloaf for a church supper or a bike gang where everybody's been busy prayin' or raisin' hell then you make a big hamloaf and cook it longer. I can't tell you any more'n that, seein' as how I don't have eyes in the back of my head. You have to use your good ham scraps, not gristle or crap, and remember that since your ham's already been cooked, you don't need to worry so much about poisinin' your guests.

Now you make a nice white sauce with mustard in it and pour it over the loaf after you cut it up and serve it. Just like you put syrup on pancakes when they're served, not when you mix up the batter, for God's sake. Don't bake your loaf in the sauce or you're in trouble. If you have a cup of white sauce, for instance, then maybe you'd add a tablespoon of dry mustard—or more, if you like mustard. Less if ya don't. I can't make all your decisions for you. Or you can make sandwiches outta the loaf if you've got fishermen. Worse thing in the world is to have to go fishin' on an empty stomach. A nice ham sandwich can keep a man from pukin' and if he does, anyway, then it won't be nothin' lost since fish gotta eat, too.

White Sauce: Melt close to four tablespoons of butter over a low fire and add up to four tablespoons of flour. Stir like crazy. Add about two cups hot milk or cream, dependin' on the state of your waistline or your wallet, and stir it and whisk it 'round and 'round until it's pretty thick but not too thick and then add your dry mustard. This makes about four cups of sauce, less if you've been tastin' it pretty liberal.

BARE BEEF BURGUNDY

You ever hear of that sayin', "Keep it simple?" Well, this is the simplest beef burgundy in the whole world and could be the best. People always ate a lot of it, anyway. Once I was demonstratin' at a wine convention. I had just one frypan and kept it on high the whole time, cookin' like crazy. I don't know how many pounds of meat walked off but it must've been quite a few since I was never asked back. When I asked somebody how come, they told me that I'd fed so many people for free that the purveyors there complained about how nobody bought any of their food. I was sorry I'd hurt their business since it wasn't ever my intention to cause trouble unless trouble oughta be caused.

First you need to get yourself good choice meat with fat marbled in it. Prime rib is good for this, only you take the ribs off first and barbecue 'em sometime. You take the fat off the top and save it for somethin' or you can give it to somebody's dog, dependin'. Sliver up your beef and throw it in a hot skillet with Vege-Sal in it. Don't put anything else in that skillet because you don't need to. When your meat is browned then throw in some good burgundy and then take it all out and hump it on plates. I'd put a big bowl of sour cream nearby so people could put that on if they wanted to. I know damn well some people put mushrooms and other fool things in, but I like my beef burgundy with just beef and burgundy and nothin' camouflagin' either one. You can put it on top of rice or noodles, if you need to stretch your meat out 'cause you're on a budget, honey.

Poultry

**"Nameless Roast Turkey
with Sageless Stuffing"**

DR. FRANCINE BRADLEY:

My friendship with Juanita began in 1973. I'd given my mother a copy of a book called *Hidden Restaurants of Northern California*. The segment at the end was a potpourri of restaurants that had been given only a paragraph or two. There was a review on Juanita's in which her place was described as having lots of inexpensive and good food but that people shouldn't be put off by hearing the owner call her pet chicken "Chickenshit." At that time I was an undergraduate in Avian Sciences at U.C. Davis, as well as a lifelong poultry fancier, and so that review caught my attention immediately.

One Saturday my mother and I decided to go and find this restaurant in Fetter's Hot Springs. We pulled into the parking area where there were a lot of motorcycles parked in front of this big white hotel with flags flying from its porch. A bunch of unsavory-looking people were milling around and my mother said, "What do you think, shall we go in?" I said, "Well, we've driven all this way and so we might as well go in and see what it's like." My mother and I have often told each other how glad we are that we didn't turn around and go away!

We walked into the foyer where we stood waiting uncertainly for a minute. Suddenly this woman, who was lying in bed in a room just off the foyer, yelled at us to come on in. We gingerly walked past the bedroom and into the dining room where someone told us to get a plate and go through the buffet line, which we did. We carried our plates to a table right next to a window, outside of which was a very large pig. The pig, bedded down comfortably on a pile of straw, was not wholly unlike Juanita lying in her bed off the foyer. We thought the effect was both odd and somehow charming.

Right then, Juanita walked into the dining room, took one look at us and hollered, "Why the hell are you sittin' over there?" We were startled to see this woman who had been in bed moments before now standing nearby telling us we shouldn't be sitting where we were sitting. We asked if there was a problem with where we'd chosen to sit and she said it was the coldest part of the dining room and that she would help us move someplace else. A little embarrassed, we insisted that we were fine where we were and she didn't need to bother about moving us anywhere, that I liked sitting next to the pig. So Juanita ambled off and in a second came back with two afghan blankets. "Well," she says, "if you're not goin' to move from this damned cold table then you might as well be covered up," and she unfolded the blankets and tucked one around my mother and then one around me.

After lunch we went upstairs and found a room with a monkey in a cage and out on the verandah cages full of doves and chickens. It was incredible and wonderful. Before we left that day, Juanita came back and started asking us questions about where we were from and what we did. I told her I was a student in Avian Sciences. At this point she started asking me chicken questions and volunteered the information that she was upset due to the recent death of one of her old cocks. I told her I would get her a replacement, which cheered her up a lot. Next time Mother and I went, I took Juanita some cocks—which is what they're properly called, not roosters—and Juanita started calling me the Rooster Lady. It was clear from the very beginning that Juanita was sincerely attracted to poultry, as I was, and not just because it gave her an excuse to walk around with a cock on her shoulder, shocking old ladies with barn-yard witticisms.

Mother and I became real Juanita groupies and started taking our friends there and anybody who came to visit us. I'm a very conservative person and I don't use bad language and I think that probably most of my friends think I'm more conservative than I really am. I have to admit that it was always very appealing to me to take people to Juanita's where I was obviously well-known and part of the gang. In behavior she seemed so different from me and I really liked that contrast and the shock value. Our official tour of Northern California always included the State Capitol, the Governor's Mansion—and Juanita's. I used to wonder if my more conservative friends would be able to handle the language and the animals and so on, but they would always just fall in love with Juanita and would rave about her and her restaurant all the way home. Part of her charm was that she could make anyone feel at home. As for her shouting at people, she knew who could take it and who couldn't and shouted accordingly. Besides, it was apparent to anyone who knew her even for a little while that her heart was as oversized as the rest of her!

After her place in Fetter's burned down, she moved around so often that at one point we lost track of where she'd gone. Somebody told me that she'd opened up a place in a certain town and so I called Information. I asked if there was a listing for Juanita and the operator said no. I guess there was enough disappointment in my voice to gain her sympathy and she said, "Are you talking about THE Juanita?" I said yes, and she told me where Juanita was now. That's when I discovered that there was a kind of

Juanita Hot-Line that kept track of where she'd wandered off to. I was so happy to find her again and things went on as they always had before, except that it seemed as if her restaurants were getting progressively more down-at-heel.

After graduation, I joined the faculty at U.C. Davis in the Department of Avian Sciences, and am the Area Poultry Farm Advisor for Northern California. I had also become Juanita's resident chicken expert. I'd get a phone call from her about some chicken catastrophe and could I come over right away, immediately? Of course I'd go to wherever she was and take a look. I remember one time I hurried over to Port Costa to find her holding a chicken in her arms but didn't have to get too close to know it was suffering from foul pox—you only need to smell that once to recognize it forever after. Juanita had taken real good care of it but it was really going fast and she was very upset that her usual remedy wasn't working. Her usual remedy was a shot of gin every once in awhile. I think she felt that if neither gin nor Bag Balm worked, the case was pretty hopeless. Actually it wasn't such a bad idea, but the chicken was beyond help. Happy, maybe, but beyond help. Besides, it was probably really old since so many of the animals and birds people unloaded on her were either aged or handicapped in some way. Juanita didn't care. She just loved 'em all.

Me too. I grew up on a ranch and have had chickens since I was four years old, starting with one I named Pantylegs. But as much as I've always loved them, I have never had a problem eating them. I love a good roast chicken and Juanita's was always delicious. Growing up on a farm taught me early that the chickens you name are not the chickens you eat. Unnamed chickens are Sunday Supper.

TWO BIRDS WITH ONE STONE CHICKEN

This is your all-around chicken you can do anything with. Now, I always used to fry chicken until Crisco got so high, and so I stopped fryin' it first before bakin' it. Take your chicken parts and wash 'em good and then let 'em sit just a minute in milk. Take your parts one by one and drop 'em into a bag of white flour, wheat germ and Vege-Sal and roll 'em around a minute before puttin' 'em on your baking sheet. Cover your pan with foil and pinch up the sides so that you won't steam your meat. Make sure to take it off before it's done so it won't come out lookin' like your ass in December.

Have your oven heated to 350 degrees and then throw in your chicken parts and let 'em bake in their own juices until they're slippin' off the bone. If you have any left over you can use it to make chicken salad or Chicken Sebastiani or sweet and sour or chicken salad. Two birds with one stone, see. If you fry your chicken it's not so useful later, especially if next day you're hungover or otherwise not interested in cookin', and then you can just slap your chicken with sauce and throw it on the table and nobody'll complain. They'd better not, anyway, if you've gone to all the trouble of makin' dinner when what you REALLY wanna do is fall asleep or go fishin'.

METHODIST ROAST CHICKEN

Another way to do chicken is just Vege-Sal it and put it in your oven and bake it as 325 degrees until it's good and done. I just hate it when chicken is pink inside. You'll know it's done when it falls off the bone or threatens to. Every Sunday at Grandmother Mitchell's house we'd have roast chicken and invite the visitin' preacher to come home with us to eat. One time there wasn't enough chicken, so us kids were told not to ask for a second piece since there wouldn't be enough to go around if we did. My uncle always carved and served up the chicken and that day he gave me my piece and then gave my cousin Jenny two pieces. I said, "Oh, Uncle, Aunt Lizzie says we can't have two pieces 'cause there won't be enough to go around!" First of all there was just quiet. Then Aunt Lizzie said, "You may leave the table now, Juanita," in that voice of hers everybody obeyed, includin' her husband and he was a millionaire. I was glad to go 'cause the table was full of aunts and uncles and cousins and that visitin' preacher and nobody knew where to look, so I was just happy to go to my room so they wouldn't all look at ME. Aunt Lizzie had kind of a speech impediment and talked through her nose, but I just loved that old lady! This millionaire she'd married, after her first husband kicked the bucket, she had that guy trained in no time flat. What Lizzie wanted, Lizzie got, even if she sounded funny when she asked for it.

SALLY STANFORD'S
TWO-ALARM CHICKEN

Okies fry chicken the same way, no matter who they are, so even though I was in charge of fryin' the chicken that day at Sally's house, she always did it the same way I did. Okies is okies, honey, no matter how many diamonds they wear. Anyway, you take your chicken and cut it up in pieces, savin' the neck and back and gizzard parts for stock or your pig, whatever comes first. Wash your parts in milk and then throw 'em in a bag with white flour, wheat germ and Vege-Sal and then set 'em down in a skillet fulla hot hot hot oil and brown 'em. Now you have a choice if ya wanna leave 'em on the stove, then you turn your fire down low until your parts are done. Or you can put 'em on a cookie sheet and bake 'em. If you're flush you can pour white wine over 'em, if the person you're cookin' for treats you right. Put a piece of foil over the top but be sure to pull up the edges so you don't steam your meat.

So this time I was at Sally's place in San Francisco where she used to be a madam but wasn't yet mayor of Sausalito, which she was afterwards. Everybody always used to say I'd been one of Sally's girls but I wasn't because Sally always said I'd never charge enough and she was right. We were in the kitchen fryin' chicken when the lights all went out and the kitchen started on fire. Took us by surprise and the chicken wasn't near done. So Sally called the Fire Department and I went to get my little kerosene lantern I'd just happened to buy that very day. I always bought lots of 'em because I liked kerosene lanterns the way other people like candles.

Now, Sally had plenty of candles but ya can't fry chicken on a candle, which goes to show that it was smarter, in the long run, to buy kerosene lanterns. This particular one fitted in a steel case so you could use it as a little stove. Sally and I went into the livin' room and got the chicken on the lantern about the same time the Fire Department arrived. They started givin' us all this crap about how we had to get out, but we told 'em we weren't about to let our chicken get cold so they could just go on about their business and not pay us any mind, so they did. They started draggin' their hoses through Sally's livin' room and as I was finishin' up the chicken she kept yellin', "Now don't you get my carpets wet!"

We had a good time and the chicken turned out just dee-licious. It was interestin' to watch the boys put out the fire and they didn't get the rugs wet, though the kitchen was another story altogether, whooeee! By the time they were packed up and ready to leave we'd just about finished, which was lucky since we needed to get some ice for our drinks.

You know, this chicken is always good, but it tasted better than usual that night, maybe because it was sorta like campin' out and cookin' over a fire—only the fire was in another room. Any food tastes better that way. Always serve your fried chicken with milk gravy or else it doesn't seem like fried chicken. Melt your butter in a pan and add flour and whisk it around and around until it's kinda brown and then add your warm milk to it and any drippins' or crusty parts from off your pan. If ya don't have any money for oil—good oil has just gone sky high—then you can try just plain roast chicken. Up to you, honey, if the damn IRS has taken all your money.

CHICKEN SEBASTIANI

August Sebastiani and I were great friends 'cause we both liked all kinda birds. He shot his sometimes, but other than that we felt about the same about 'em. He used to come by and tell me to jump in his pickup and come look at some new birds he had, some kinda swans or pigeons or somethin', and sometimes I would and sometimes I wouldn't, dependin' on my mood. He'd come into my place dressed in his striped overalls and eat at the kitchen table with the help. His son, Sam, he'd come with him, too, sometimes. I had two round oak tables in my kitchen and they'd be fulla local folk, eatin' my food. He had a good appetite, which I always liked in a man. I never have liked a man's appetite BEST, but it's always come in second. August really liked my chicken so it's nice to name it after him. Down to earth guy, fulla beans.

What you do is, you take your Two Stone Chicken and you strip the skin off it. You can do this with raw chicken, too, but I always used leftover for my Chicken Sebastiani, if I had it. Then you pour your sauce over it and heat 'em up together in your oven at the same time so it doesn't turn to poison while your back's turned. You can't be too careful with chicken. Take one gallon of chopped onions and fry it in a pan fulla butter with one gallon of chopped celery and one dozen green peppers, chopped real fine. Add 3 - #10 cans of tomato sauce and 2 - #10 cans of fruit juice, any kinda Italian herbs you like, and sauterne wine. Bring all this stuff to a boil and then let it sit there simmerin' for two or three hours. You can make less than this, if ya want to, or you can make a big bunch up ahead and eat lotsa chicken done this way. It's good cold, too, if your kids don't object to takin' it to school. I never could understand peanut butter and jelly but then I never had kids. I always said I enjoyed the procedure without the production. You can use white wine instead of sauterne or you could leave it out altogether, which August wouldn't have appreciated at all, honey.

FAIRWEATHER CHICKEN
(Sometimes Sweet and Sometimes Sour)

This is one of the chicken dishes you can make with your Two Birds with One Stone Chicken—that is if you roasted yourself two chickens in the first place. You can also make this with raw chicken, but why bother when you can make it with chicken leftover from a couple nights before and nobody'll know the difference? So, what you do is, you mix up four tablespoons of cider vinegar with four tablespoons of tomato paste and four tablespoons of soy sauce and a little ground ginger, if you feel like it. Some people hate ginger and some people love it and since you can't tell which one's which you're better off not puttin' too much in. Pour in the syrup from two 16 ounce cans of pineapple chunks. Put this on your stove over a low fire and cook until it's hot, then add a large chopped onion and a large green pepper that you've fried just a minute in butter until they're limp as a day old flapjack. Put your chicken in a pan and heat it up. Then stir into your sauce cornstarch mixed in water to thicken it up and when it's right, throw in your pineapple chunks. Pour your sauce over your chicken and let it marry up awhile before you serve it on rice. You don't have to serve it on rice but you need somethin' to soak up the sauce and rice makes it seem kinda Chinese. Bread strikes me wrong, and noodles do, too. Better stick with rice and forget it.

PICKLED CHICKEN INNARDS

I used to get all these gizzards and hearts and livers from my chicken butcher and what I'd do is, I'd poach 'em in water with picklin' spice in it until they were done, and then drain 'em and marinate 'em in oil and vinegar for maybe a day. I used to put 'em out on my buffet inside the bottom part of this cookie jar that was shaped like a chicken only with its head off, innards where the innards were. I didn't have this on my buffet all the time since the butcher'd run out of 'em and we'd have to wait until people had bought enough outside chicken for there to be a lotta INSIDE chicken. I guess they looked a lot like little turds, but people just loved 'em! Cats liked 'em, too, but when I made 'em for my cats I left off the marinade part since cats aren't generally too happy about salad dressin'. Dogs aren't so particular, in my experience.

NAMELESS TURKEY WITH SAGELESS STUFFING

I'll never forget the Thanksgivin' that a friend of mine gave me a turkey, a big white one. I didn't want any of my customers to think I'd cooked her so I served steak and kept the turkey for a pet. You can't eat anythin' you name, and sometimes you can't eat anythin' you don't know the name of, either. Pets aren't food any more'n people are. This was when I was in that old ferryboat, the Charles Van Damme. Poor thing laid two dud eggs in the phone booth we had on deck for ballast and, since I didn't want any frustrated females on board, I went on up to a hatchery and bought two fertile eggs and slipped 'em in on her, unawares. Two cocks hatched out, but one of 'em lost his balance and fell down the stairs. Maybe they both had dropsy, or somethin', 'cause his brother always used to fall overboard and we'd have to send somebody out to rescue 'im in a dinghy. He lived with us five years until one Christmas Day some woman walked out with him under her fur coat, pretendin' he was a muff. Never did trust women wearin' fur coats. They used to just get my goat when they'd let 'em trail all over my floor, pickin' up the sawdust I put down there on purpose. I'd tell 'em not to mess up my floor that way and if they didn't mind their ways I'd throw 'em out, coat an' all. Once this uppity little broad came in wearin' a mink and gave me a hard time for servin' the fishermen first. So I said, "Fine," I said, "then I'll serve YOU first," and rubbed mustard in her coat as a kind of appetizer.

Always use fresh turkeys unless frozen is on sale cheaper. One time all these turkeys arrived the day before Thanksgivin', frozen hard as big rocks. Barbara, the gal that played her mandolin in my place, we carted the turkeys over to my bathroom and threw 'em in the bathtub under the shower. We kept turnin' 'em and turnin' 'em until they was thawed out enough to be roasted next day. Not that I'm recommendin' this as a cookin' method, soakin' before roastin', but it sure worked that day. "To survive is to connive" is one of my mottos, honey!

I usually liked usin' Willie Bird turkeys out there on Stage Gulch Road. You can use other kinds, too, but in these parts Willie Bird is best. I'd wash him first and run water through his neck and wash his ass good and pat him nice and dry. Then I'd put foil in a roaster pan and put 'im on top of the foil and throw 'im in the oven at 325 degrees, washed but plain as plain. Once that bird got goin', I'd baste him with melted butter and then, after awhile, suck up the juices from the pan and baste him with that every once in awhile. Don't put your Vege-Sal on until your turkey has a good start in life and don't use anythin' but Vege-Sal. I never ever used white salt except when I was boilin' eggs or when I poured it on my grill and wiped it off to clean off the crap. Otherwise, white salt does not have house room in any kitchen of mine and shouldn't in yours, either. I never never never put on pepper because that's individual choice and not up to me. You want pepper, goody for you. You don't want pepper—well, honey, nobody's gonna force it down your throat. After the first basting, I'd always put on a good clean piece of cheese-cloth and baste over that until the bird's done.

My turkey stuffin' was always popular, especially with vegetarians who couldn't have any turkey and didn't wanna sit there on Thanksgiving with a plate fulla creamed onions. What you do is, the night before you fry up your chopped onions and celery and let that get cold before you mix it into your crumbled up bread and English muffins. If you add it hot to your bread it'll come out gummy and gooey. Now, when I made my dressin', I'd put in two and a half dozen eggs, but unless you have a real big family you won't need nearly that much. Beat up however many eggs you need and stir that in to sorta glue everything together, then pour in your potato water or vegetable water until it's good and sloppy but not TOO sloppy. Then you add lots and lots of butter on top and put it in your oven to bake the last hour with your turkey. I always always always baked my stuffin' separately so nobody would die in case it went bad. Nobody was ever sick in any of my restaurants, so do as I do and as I say, both. Never never never add sage. I hate sage in dressing and when you taste how good dressin' is without sage you'll never wanna put it in again.

Thanksgivin' always has good memories for me because we always went to my grandmother's house in Hominy. She always spring-cleaned the week before so everything would be nice for the holidays, and so I got in the habit of doin' that, too. Now, at home, I just drop everything behind my couches, "outta sight, outta mind," but they never did allow couches in restaurants so there wasn't anyplace to hide my junk in the good old days. A couch comes in mighty handy sometimes, if you catch my drift.

Casseroles

"Beauty Shop Spaghetti"

DR. PHILIP RASHID:

I was stationed at Travis Air Force Base, an officer and an oral surgeon. I'd heard a lot about Juanita's restaurant so a bunch of us officers decided to go one night. We piled in the car and when we got to El Verano her place was packed and with a long line waiting to get in. Juanita suddenly walked past and saw these men in uniform at the end of the line. She insisted we come in first and told a waitress to take us into the "make points room" which turned out to be her bedroom. She ordered someone to go get a card table and three chairs which were set up beside her bed and with the bed as the fourth chair. We were brought all this food and enough prime rib for the whole Air Force Base. Juanita kept poking in her head and hollering something and we'd holler back, having the most wonderful time. After awhile she came in and said, "All right, move your butts over." I wondered kind of nervously what was next but she just pulled back the covers, climbed in bed and went immediately to sleep.

Usually we asked to eat in Juanita's bedroom, but one Sunday brunch when we were eating in the dining room, Juanita came sashaying in like Queen Julianna, looking really quite regal in her muumuu and mantilla comb, and with her rooster on her shoulder. Only there was this big blob of turkey crap on her huge bottom. She shouted, "Somebody stole my cock but guess what? My neighbor is so nice that he gave me his!" The place broke up, of course, the officers just beating their hands on the table.

I remember one night when Juanita was expecting a large group of people from the telephone company. Something strange had happened to her employees,

I guess, and by the time I'd arrived with a friend for dinner she was just wild. The minute she saw us she yelled, "Get your asses in here and help me!" She asked me to help set this great big table with a lace tablecloth and her good china and crystal, while the dinner party milled around, watching and waiting. All of a sudden Juanita decided something was wrong with how the table was placed and she tugged at it. It collapsed. Everything broke. We picked up the corners of the tablecloth and carried everything off to the dumpster, with Juanita highly amused by the catastrophe. You never knew quite how she was going to react to something, but she was often surprising. Those telephone people said it was the best dinner they'd ever eaten. I guess the floor show made up for all the time they'd had to wait!

By the time Juanita got to Winters, she was having a hard time keeping her head above water. One night I went over to her place and every table was covered with dirty dishes and the kitchen sink was piled skyhigh. Not only had the dishwasher not shown up, but the cook and waitress hadn't either. Maybe they all quit or all got drunk. At any rate, Juanita was so glad to see me and asked if I would help her. I told her I wouldn't bus the tables or wash the dishes but I would agree to cook. That was fine with her, except that there wasn't very much to cook WITH except for lots of leftover bread. Lots and lots of leftover bread, because there was a lot of bread to begin with. There was this old fashioned stove in the middle of the dining room in Winters and that's where she'd bake the bread, right in the midst of all the hullabaloo, and then she'd put the loaves into an antique record player cabinet to keep warm, more or less. Then, when she'd serve it up, she'd serve the loaves on armrests from old school desks so customers could slice the bread at their own tables. She'd tell people the right way to carve the bread so it wouldn't squash down and get gummy, but when they didn't do it the way she said she'd come roaring back yelling, "You don't ruin my bread that way!" Then she'd slice it herself, all the time giving the people a tongue-lashing. Sometimes she'd butter the bread after she'd sliced it, figuring they'd probably do *that* wrong, too. Once these two young men started throwing their loaf of bread back and forth in the dining room like it was a football. Juanita let out a yell and the two men started running, Juanita in hot pursuit with a butcher knife in her hand. Down the street they went, Juanita yelling, "I'll teach YOU to treat my bread like that!"

Anyway, back to that crazy night; I found some pork steaks that maybe wouldn't have lasted another day and I put those on the grill with lots of garlic. Then I took a huge iron skillet she had and poured oil into it and chopped up cabbage and threw that in and fried it until it was almost burny-brown and then turned the heat down and let it simmer, during which time I made Juanita's Smashed Hash Browns. While I was doing all of this, Juanita was clearing tables and letting customers in and was taking what I cooked as soon as I'd cooked it and was putting it on the buffet where it just disappeared. I kept cooking like mad. As the night wore, on, though, Juanita started ordering me around like I was working for maybe a thousand dollars an hour and then called me a son of a bitch into the bargain. By this time we were standing there in the kitchen shaking knives at each other. Finally I said, "I don't have to take this, you know!" and I tore off my apron and threw it on the floor and made tracks. She came running after me, pleading that she didn't mean to say what she'd said and wouldn't I please please please come back. So I did.

You know, it wouldn't matter how much you did for her, she would still act toward you just as naturally as she'd act to anybody else. Once I made reservations for Easter morning brunch. When we arrived there was not only no Juanita to be found but also no tables were set and no food was cooking. I looked around and looked around and finally found her out in the yard hiding Easter eggs. I said, "Juanita! What in the hell are you doing? You have customers!" She said, "Can't you see I'm busy? I gotta get these eggs all out before any kids get here! If you want breakfast go cook it yourself!" I was furious because I'd brought so many people with me and all of us were hungry, but I rolled up my sleeves and got things going and pretty soon Juanita sailed into the kitchen, smiling and happy, and as if there wasn't anything unusual about a restaurateur out hiding Easter eggs while the customers were doing the cooking. In her world, I guess, that's the way things are supposed to be.

CATHOUSE LASAGNE

This little old Italian lady used to come by the hotel where I'd just opened my restaurant after the last one'd burnt down. She was scared to say peep 'cause she thought I was runnin' some sorta cathouse, which I never would've gotten myself involved with since runnin' a restaurant had enough problems. After awhile I got her sorta cornered and herded her up on the porch to meet my mother and I guess she figured I couldn't be runnin' a cathouse if my mother was in the place. First she just made it to the porch, and then to the lobby and then all the way into the kitchen where my "girls" were peelin' potatoes and forkin' muffins. I figured since she was in the kitchen I might as well ask her, since she was Italian, did she know how to make lasagne? She showed me how and it's not much different from spaghetti only your noodles are different and you don't put all your sauce on top. At first she made it for us, herself, but after awhile I had to take over when her daughter put her in a rest home, which was a pretty lousy thing to do, especially since she died.

What you do is, you make your lasagne noodles and your spaghetti sauce. Grease your casserole real good and then put on a layer of noodles, a layer of sauce, a layer of noodles, a layer of sauce, a layer of noodles, a layer of sauce and so on until you run out of one or the other and then stop. You can put ricotta cheese on top of the noodles each time if you want but make sure you end up with sauce on top. Then you can sprinkle the top with grated Parmesan cheese, so it's more Italian, and then bake it until it's done. You'll know it's done because the edges will be bubblin' and it just looks done. Put foil on the top so it won't dry out but take it off right before the end to sorta brown up the top. Beer is good with lasagne, too, but not inside the sauce, inside YOU—unless you haven't been behavin' too good, and then you better stick with ice tea.

EGGPLANT DINGHIES

This is another dish Dr. Rashid used to make for our buffet every once in awhile. These little dinghies would always disappear off the buffet table like a tornado'd struck.

What you do first is, you take your nice big eggplant, a shiny one and with none of those little rotten places. You cut the stem end off and save it for the animals. Then you cut the eggplant you got left lengthwise in four sections and then cut those sections into halves so you got eight long pieces like french fries only fatter. Cut those eight in half and then salt 'em and let 'em sit there and bleed until they run outta juice or you run outta patience waitin'.

Get your skillet real hot and then pour in your oil. Wipe off the eggplant with paper towels and throw 'em into the skillet and brown 'em fast on each side, real quick, and then take 'em out and let 'em sit there all lined up on paper towels until they're cool enough so you won't burn your fingers too bad. Cut a pocket almost the whole length of each piece of eggplant, bein' real careful not to cut all the way through the skin so your filling will fall out on the floor and you have to start the whole damn business all over again.

Meanwhile you're frying in a skillet some chopped pecans in butter. You take the nuts out when they're goldy brown and leave 'em sit. Then you either grind yourself or chop up in tiny pieces a pound or so of ground round. Itty bitty cubes, I'm talkin' about here, not big friggin' chunks. Turn the fire up and throw in the meat and turn it fast so it doesn't lose its juice and then you throw in some chopped onions and pull your skillet off the fire and mix in the pecans.

Now you get yourself a tablespoon and you stuff the little dinghies but not so much that they slop over. Full, though, or else they'll sort of collapse in on themselves and you'll have yourself a skillet full of eggplant mush. Then you take a small can of peeled tomatoes and a little tomato sauce and you pour all this into a baking dish and put on top of that your eggplant dinghies and then sprinkle garbonzo beans around like they're little round people that've fallen outta the dinghies. You can bake this covered in your oven or you can cover it and simmer it on top of your stove if it's summertime and hot as hell already. After awhile you take the cover off, if you got it in the oven, and let the tops brown real nice. I can't tell you just exactly how long it takes to bake but I guess about as long as you can stand smelling them cook, maybe about forty-five minutes.

The Doctor always liked to serve Lebanese rice with this, and you can do that or you can fix yourself some noodles or potatoes done any which way, because potatoes are always good no matter how you treat 'em. Like nuns, if you catch my drift.

RICE À LA RASHID

You take spaghetti or vermicelli and break it up a little in your hands and brown it in butter. Then in a pan you mix water and butter and a big pinch of Vege-Sal and let it come to a boil and then throw in your rice that you've soaked for a couple of hours, but you have to drain it first. Put your browned spaghetti (or vermicelli or whatever) on top of that and let it simmer for half an hour. We used to serve that a lot in Sausalito, even before I knew Dr. Rashid, because we had this cook for awhile that was Lebanese. We called her "Little Bit" since she always wanted to cook little tiny batches of everything and, besides, she was pretty short. Not a dwarf, or anything, but kinda small. One of my fawns, Sissy, used to butt her into the refrigerator, but that was because Little Bit wouldn't give her the green onions Sissy just loved. She shoulda looked both ways before bending over, but some people are like that. Even though she thought of the rice first I'm callin' this rice after Dr. Rashid since he came up with the Eggplant Dinghies. Fair is fair.

BEAUTY SHOP SPAGHETTI

There's nothin' like a big plate a' spaghetti when you're just too pooped to pop. You don't have to cut it with a knife, either. Matter of fact, if you're REAL tired, all ya have to do is put your face down close to your plate and just start shovelin' and pretty soon the noodles will come taggin' along by themselves and all you have to do is suck and swallow. Well, you have to chew a little, too, or ya might choke to death.

Spaghetti is simple. That's why kids learn to make it and most men. You fry up your good ground chuck until it's brown. For ten pounds of chuck you add 3/4 gallon of chopped onions you've already fried up. Throw in to your onions two bunches of chopped parsley. Mix this up good, then add your drained meat, Vege-Sal, pepper, Italian seasoning like basil and oregano. Mix this up good and then add two gallons of tomato puree, one and a half gallons of water, and mix this up good, too. Let this sit on the back of your stove over a low fire for maybe three hours and then add chopped up fresh basil for the last ten minutes of cookin' time. Boil yourself up some spaghetti noodles, maybe five packages, and there you are. This probably serves about twenty people, unless they been out huntin' or fishin', and then it might serve fifteen.

Back in Sausalito, I used to go across the street to this beauty parlor. I never did go for my hair, since my hair tended to stay on my head by itself, but I went over 'cause I felt just so damn sorry for those poor broads under the dryers. I'd bring along big platters of spaghetti and french bread and I'd plonk 'em down on their laps and tell 'em to eat every bite, 'cause they needed all the strength they could get, sittin' under those hot dryers all day long. I know they were choosin' to do that under their own free will, but you can't condemn people when they don't know any better. Even fools gotta eat.

NAKED SPAGHETTI

When I was a kid in Oklahoma, sometimes we didn't have anythin' to eat but spaghetti with nothin' on it. Looked just like worms, but when you're hungry you'll eat just about anything, honey. Later on sometimes I had to serve plain naked spaghetti 'cause somebody'd stolen all the food. Like once this buncha kids came in on a Sunday mornin'. Then they went out into the parkin' lot and started up a brouhaha that turned out to be more ha ha than brou, if you catch my drift. We all went runnin' out to break it up and while we were out there with our backs turned, a bunch of 'em went in the back door to the kitchen and just cleaned me out; hamburger, prime ribs, ham, everything. When we finally went on back in, I didn't have any meat to serve anyone whatsoever. California Meat sent his men down for Sunday night so I could stay open, but before that we just flipped our lids tryin' to find a thing to feed people with since all we had was beans beans beans, spaghetti noodles and maybe some potato salad. Cops couldn't catch the kids that did it, either, so I didn't even have the satisfaction of tellin' them to their faces what I thought of shenanigans like that. Whooeee, would they've gotten an earful! Customers mainly just waited around all day until suppertime, shootin' pool and gettin' a little drunk, maybe, what with the meat stolen an' all.

Another time these cops watched a man steal two of my prime ribs and they followed him home and caught 'im. That might've been nice for the cops but it didn't help me one damn bit since who wants to eat prime ribs that've been manhandled for five city blocks? At the hotel one day someone stole two platters full of stuffed eggs and we took off after 'im. Wasn't too hard findin' where he'd run to since he left a trail of eggs behind him. One thief I got pinned under a chair in the dinin' room but I wasn't always that lucky. One day this guy stole two forty pound cheeses and a whole prime rib that had already been cooked.

Somebody told me what he was doin', but when I went out after 'im and looked in his car I forgot to check the back seat and lost the cheese. I guess he was havin' a party and didn't feel like doin' any of the cookin' himself. I understand that, honey, havin' felt like that more'n a few hundred times myself.

If ya wanna jazz up your noodles, add minced up garlic and some butter. You can sauté the garlic first in butter for the crybabies, but raw garlic is better for cleanin' up any lingerin' colds you got comin' on.

MARGE'S ENCHILADDIES

I named these for Marge since she started makin' 'em in the Galley in Sausalito longer ago than I care to think about right now, thank you very much. I made 'em just like Marge did except she says she used to boil up her onions and then pour the onion water into the sauce and if I'd caught her doin' that I'd have slapped her good. I always poured the onion water into my beans because beans make ya fart anyway, so it doesn't matter.

So many people loved our enchiladdies we just couldn't keep enough of 'em on the buffet 'cause they'd disappear like a pack a' dogs had been through the place. There was this actress, Juanita Brown, who was in San Francisco doin' "South Pacific" for some reason and she was just dyin' for some of our enchiladdies. So one day I made a bunch of 'em and some chili and took it all over to where she was stayin' in a suite in the St. Francis Hotel. Poor thing, she was just all tuckered out from her actin' and havin' to eat that uptown crap and those enchiladdies perked her up plenty.

We used to buy these great handmade tortillas seven or eight dozen at a time in this place in San Francisco, sometimes corn and sometimes flour, we weren't real religious about it. They was thick and good-sized. The place we bought 'em at opened a closer outlet after awhile but it got closed down 'cause of the rats, so we had to keep goin' into the city. It was worth it, though, 'cause those tortillas just were better tastin', for some reason, than any others we tried.

Chop up a' buncha yellow onions, cover 'em with water and simmer 'em for awhile. Drain off the water to save for your beans and put the onions somewhere. Fry up your ground chuck until it's brown. Add Grandma's Chili Seasoning to your meat and a pinch or two of chili pepper flakes, however much you think your family can stand, and toss in some comino you've rubbed first between your hands so it's got less stems and more oomph. Pour your onions in last and mess 'em around with everything else and that part's done.

You can make enchiladdy sauce if ya want but it's easier just to buy it. Open your can and pour it in a bowl. Then you fry up your tortillas in a little hot oil to make 'em soft enough to do what you want with 'em, but boy! You have to be careful with your hands or you're gonna go through Bag Balm like crazy. I didn't never mind burnin' my fingers in a good cause, but sometimes you get tired of it. Dip your tortilla in your sauce and put it down in your bakin' pan. Put some meat on top and sprinkle on some grated cheddar cheese and a whole black pitted olive and roll it up. We only just put whole black olives in because if somebody didn't like olives then they could just spit it out. This is much easier on everybody than havin' somebody pick through your enchiladdy for bits of olive like a pig rootin' through garbage. Boy, I just couldn't stand people eatin' MY food that way! Keep doin' this until ya run outta tortillas or meat or both, then stop. Pour your sauce on over your enchiladdies and dump the rest of your cheese on top of that and some chopped up green onions. Cover your pan with foil so they don't all dry up on you while they're cookin'. Should take maybe 45 minutes at 325 degrees, or less time in a hotter oven, whatever.

CABBAGE WEENIES

This was Dr. Rashid's recipe and he used to make this for our buffet sometimes when he felt like it. He was just a great dentist and a great guy and, boy, could he cook! Almost as good as me, only not quite.

Anyways, what you do is you take this ground round, as much as you think you'll need, maybe a pound or more if you're just gonna make enough for yourself and some leftover to share. If you're gonna make this for a whole lot of people then you'd better double and triple everything one or two times over so you won't run out. Nothin' spoils a nice dinner like runnin' outta food. You can also use round steak all cut up small or sirloin or whatever you can afford to buy and still have enough money left to be able to stop in at a yard sale on the way home from the store. You melt a stick of butter to a cup of cooked rice. You pour the hot butter on top of the rice so it soaks it up like little sponges and then you put on your Vege-Sal and pepper and cinnamon, as much as you like. Dr. Rashid likes a lot of cinnamon, a whole teaspoon, but you can do what you like in your own home.

You mix that up and after it cools down you throw in your meat. If you don't wait until the rice cools down your meat will turn a sort of sickly-lookin' white and you don't want to do that. You cut the core out of a big-enough cabbage and you steam it over boiling water and then take the leaves off fast, before they get all wilted. Your fingers might get burned some but it's all in a good cause and if you have an aloe plant or some Bag Balm on your sink you can take care of any burns you get after you've finished makin' the weenies.

Open up a leaf and then put in it maybe a tablespoon of your meat mixture and roll it up like a fifty cent cigar and lay it down in your baking dish. Keep it up, honey, until you've run out of one or the other, cabbage leaves or meat, and you can eat what you have left on the counter, if you want, or throw it in some soup. After you get all this done, you chop yourself some garlic and sprinkle it on top—don't worry about your breath because your health is more important and what's worse, a bad cold or a fairweather friend? You can also throw in the leftover cabbage, if you're not hungry, only you have to break it up into pieces first. You don't want anything to go to waste, especially if you don't have a pig. I don't have a pig anymore myself, but I got cats that eat like pigs so it don't matter.

Then you mix up a tablespoon of tomato paste in some water and toss in two or three beef bouillon cubes and melt everything into the water and then add the juice of half a lemon and pour that on top of the weenies so it just covers 'em but not drowns 'em. You put a dish on top of the weenies so they won't roll around and fall apart while they're cookin'. Then you set the dish to simmer on top of the stove, covered with a lid and let it cook some while. About halfway through you take the lid off and set it halfway on and halfway off and cook the weenies some more, only you turn down the heat so it simmers real gentle until you figure it's done. The bottom of the weenies should be kind of brown, which you just have to figure hit or miss since you can't tell without takin' the whole damn thing apart to see.

BOOKKEEPER'S SPECIAL FETTUCINE

Micki Smircich came up with this one for our buffet and it always got wolfed right down. Micki did her best with what she had to work with, but sometimes she was just fed up with me because we seemed to run outta money kinda often, especially if there was a real good yard sale or the Church Mouse thrift shop got somethin' in I just couldn't resist. Since this recipe doesn't call for meat, it's cheaper to make and people don't usually eat three pounds of it like they did with my prime rib. Bookkeeper's life can be just hell, sometimes, when the books don't add up or there isn't any money left to pay the bills, and so maybe this was Micki's way of balancin' our checkbook.

First you cook and drain 8 ounces of fettucine noodles. Mix this up with eight ounces of cubed cream cheese, three ounces of grated Parmesan cheese, half a cup of oleo and half a cup of milk. Do it fast or your noodles will go all stiff on ya and nothin' will melt together and what you'll end up with is glop. This only serves maybe two people, or three if one's a kid, but Micki gave me this recipe and she's one of those real thin people you can't ever believe eat anything at all.

HOT TAMALE PIE

First thing is, you boil off your onions and do whatever with the water. First thing in the mornin', a nice big glass of onion water and by noon you'll be up and at 'em. Generally you don't make tamale pie for breakfast, but maybe you can do your onions ahead of time and have a jump on your day. Fry your ground chuck brown and add your onions and cook that for awhile to marry 'em up a little. Then you make yourself a batch of cornmeal mush and line your bakin' dish with some of it. Then you put on a layer of meat and some canned enchilada sauce and more mush, meat and enchilada sauce, like that. Make sure you have enough sauce to finish off the top or your top layer of mush'll be tough as week-old sourdough. Sprinkle the top with cheddar cheese—you can put cheese inside, too, if you remember. Pitted black olives chopped up are good, too, if nobody hates olives and you remember to put in the pitted kind. If you don't, there'll be hell to pay somewhere along the line. Once one of my girls put 'em in unpitted and when we found out I had to run into my dinin' room and yell, "Spit your olives out RIGHT NOW!" You could hear this ping! ping! ping! as everybody did. I like to have murdered that idiot, but what're ya gonna do? You gotta read labels, not just throw in any damn thing you want. I used to put in hominy, too, if I remembered. I just love hominy in the worst way, maybe 'cause my dear Grandma lived there.

CHILI RELLENOS O LAY

I was always known for my rellenos and you will be, too. Somebody cut down this recipe from fifty servings to maybe six, but you can multiply it back up to fifty if you want to go to all that trouble. I never did see the sense in cookin' for six since then you don't have any leftovers to speak with and if you're too hungover next day to cook there won't be nothin' left in your fridge and you'll have to order in a pizza or tell everybody to go to hell.

Beat up a cup of half and half with two eggs and a quarter cup of flour. Beat beat beat until you can't beat it no more and then stop. Split open 3 - 4 oz. cans of whole green chilis, rinse out your seeds and drain. Set these somewhere and then grate up half a pound of Monterey Jack cheese and likewise with half a pound of sharp cheddar. Mix up your cheese but keep half a cup for your top. Then what you do is, you make layers in your casserole dish, puttin' in chilis, egg, cheese, chili, eggs, cheese until you run out. Then pour one eight ounce can of tomato sauce over the top and sprinkle your cheese all over. Put your casserole in your oven at 350 degrees and keep it there for about one and a quarter hours. This isn't one of those recipes that's better the next day, but if you're by yourself or feelin' lousy it can taste just dandy, along with a good cold beer if you're not on the wagon.

BURNED OUT, DOWN 'N OUT, FOUR-ALARM CHILI

After my second place burned down, in Fetter's Hot Springs, we had about twelve people without water or 'lectricity or nothin' much at all. First we got water hooked up and then I started cookin' on a wood stove that we'd saved from the hotel porch, draggin' it off while all these firemen are tellin' us to get outta their way. Lucky we did because we mighta starved otherwise. We all sort of camped and slept in the nearby cabins or wherever and the animals had to take potluck in the bushes. I remember standin' out there in the spring sunshine, cookin' in an old raggedy muumuu and with a blanket 'round my shoulders and no shoes at all—this was why I burnt my feet so bad, walkin' through the cinders so they still aren't right even to this day. The pig and chickens and pigeons and everybody just wandered around kinda blank-like, except now they could come into the kitchen anytime they wanted to until we finally got 'em penned up. It was a hell of an upsettin' time but I was too damned busy to think about everything I'd lost. Hungry people can take your mind off things like that.

One thing I remember cookin' was chili. This fills people up and if it's hot enough they'll feel full for a lot longer. I never did make my food too hot, though, just enough to give it zip but not set fire to anybody's tongue. We'd had enough of fires, anyway, for awhile. I always boil my onions until they're soft and then save the water for somethin' else where gas is no consideration. Chili is iffy enough without gas. If ya feel a cold comin' on, you should drink the onion water right down or give it to someone who will. Fry your ground chuck about the same time your onions are boilin' and then add the onions to the meat after the onions are drained and meat's brown. Then add however much canned tomatoes. I never did use stringy meat or tomato sauce in my chili and you don't have to, either. Then put in however much Grandma's Chili Seasoning you think everybody can stand. What I always did is, I always served beans on the side so people could add 'em to their chili if they wanted the challenge of it and if they wanted to steer clear, then they could. Chili is good with hominy added to it and beer, if you have some left over. Nice thing about this recipe is you can add however much you want of everything and if a few more people than you thought show up at your house you can just throw in some more tomatoes or open another can of beans. Tortillas is good with chili, too, and you can put on some cheddar cheese if you have to.

Fish

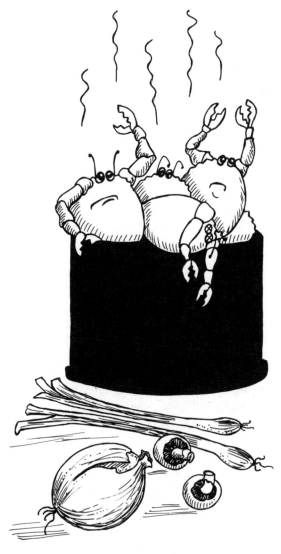

"Barely Dead Crab Cioppino"

MARGE TURNAUER:

In 1957, my union told me I was to go over to Juanita's Galley for a job interview. I'd read about Juanita in Herb Caen's column and I said, "What do ya have against me to send me there?" She had a · reputation of being kinda tough to work for. They said, "Oh, you'll get along with her fine." I went over on the Saturday and was interviewed by her husband who told me that for breakfast they'd go through 45 pounds of sausage and 50 pounds of bacon and about 20 hams and so many pounds of potatoes and so many cases of eggs and I thought to myself, "Who is this guy foolin'?" I'd cooked breakfast in restaurants for many years and thought he was pullin' my leg. He told me to come to work next morning, which just happened to be Easter Sunday, Juanita's busiest day of the year.

I got there about eight o'clock to find that Juanita had colored cases and cases of eggs and all of 'em with the names of customers and their kids on 'em. She spent all day handing these eggs out to everybody and not forgettin' a single person. Then there was this incubator in the corner of the dining room full of chicks poppin' outta their shells. This doctor had a paper thumbtacked to the wall and every time a chick hatched he'd mark it down and sign his name as Attending Physician. Dick turned out to be right. We went through everything, all the bacon and ham and sausage and what seemed like thousands of English muffins. I didn't get outta there until three o'clock and I tell you I was draggin'. They said, "See you in the mornin'" and I thought, "Oh, God, not again!" But I went back, all right, and went on workin' for her for ten years, off and on. Great years, too. Lively, if you know what I mean.

Breakfast usually stopped about two o'clock when the fishermen would come in. Then we'd start cookin' hamburgers. On English muffins, the best things you'd ever want to eat. She used ground chuck and they had to be cooked no more than medium rare. If you ordered burgers any more done than medium you might get it but sometimes you'd wish you hadn't 'cause it would arrive with a lotta lip. If you ordered "VVR" you were great. "VR" and you were fine. "M" was okay. But if you ordered "VVD"—what she called Very Very Dead—this was enough to get ya thrown out wearin' your burger in your pants. Juanita would say and do anything she felt like. People loved her—and hated her, too—because of that. But, I tell you, you always knew where you stood with her every second, and you can't say that about too many people. Most people are too two-faced for that. But not Juanita. Husbands always liked her, wives not nearly so much because some of their husbands liked Juanita a little TOO much, if ya know what I mean. They were real attracted to her because she was such a real person. Generous to a fault, too.

I have to admit, service was pretty slow most of the time, mainly because the place was so busy and the kitchen wasn't really big enough to handle the crowd. I still have dreams that I'm back at Juanita's Galley and can't seem to get through all those piled up food orders and Juanita's somewhere in the background, screamin' and carryin' on. Some people would put these awful names on the tops of their orders and Juanita or a waitress would be in the dining room, shouting out these horrible names and everybody would holler and laugh.

Things would be a hell of a lot slower if Juanita was in the kitchen, since she'd stand around in those gold, high-heeled wedgies she always wore, yakkin' with anybody that came near. I was too damn busy most of the time to notice anybody at all. The Kingston Trio came in for two years with their little blue flight bags and I still thought they worked for Pan Am. Lots of famous people came in, though I mostly didn't get to see 'em. Mort Sahl and Johnny Winters and Sterling Hayden and Glenn Ford—that doll—but I missed most of that action. I remember the time Johnny Winters came in and next day he climbed the mast of the Balclutha sailing ship, stark naked.

Herb Caen always gave Juanita a lot of plugs. And sometimes he unplugged her, too, like the time he wrote that her place looked like a Goodwill store and our take went down about two hundred dollars. But Juanita didn't care. Everything was all right with her. She thought the same about everyone, whether they were plain folks or Indian chief, it didn't matter to her at all. She treated 'em all the same and she expected her help to, too.

Not long after I started workin' for her, Juanita got one of the fawns she often adopted and kept around the place. Usually they'd be found by the highway patrol near where their mothers had been killed by a car and the patrolman would bring it on over. Juanita always named the fawns "Sissy," one after another. They'd sleep under the grill or under the tables and sometimes you'd have these babes come in all dressed up after a night on the town, sittin' there snooty-like. All of a sudden they'd let out a scream 'cause Sissy would've peed on their shoes. He'd pee on their shoes or turn around in front of 'em and drop a tail of little marbles. They were the cutest little fawns! Once there was this one fawn that hated a girl who worked for Juanita for awhile. She was Armenian and she used to make this lamb dish outta lamb she'd let rot in marinade for days. It'd smell to high heaven but everybody liked it. Anyway, she was mean and wouldn't give that Sissy any green onions, which he loved. She'd open up the refrigerator to get somethin' out and once she was bent over, Sissy would run over and butt her in the ass and she'd fly head first into the crisper. Once she hit her head and sued Juanita and won, as I remember, but she just kept on workin' for her, though. Sometimes one of the fawns would stand up on its hind legs and lap at the flapjack batter, but there wasn't anything bad about that. Fawns are probably cleaner than most people, I'll bet.

Juanita loved kids like she loved animals. I remember once she went over to the city and bought a station wagon full of toys for about forty kids she knew, mine included. This was when she was goin' through her divorce and she charged it all to Dick. She was always doin' nice things for people. Once she spent three months taking care of Sally Stanford in her bordello after she'd had a heart attack. I was surprised she had a heart, she was such a tough cookie.

'Course, Juanita could be pretty tough herself. One night she called me to come over, that some guys had vandalized her place and broken a lotta dishes and wrecked the kitchen. I went over to help her clean up and there she was with a quart of Scotch. Boy, did she get loaded! Got into a fight with two guys in the parkin' lot, brothers who showed up with these big dogs. She started readin' 'em the riot act over somethin' or another. They go into their car and started to drive away but Juanita just held on, held on and didn't give a damn that they were draggin' her halfway across the parkin' lot, raggin' at 'em the whole time. Finally she fell off. Wandered back on in, talkin' to herself, mad as hell. Actually, most of the time, all that happened when she drank was that she just got sharper. She always said what she meant, sober or drunk, and meant it just the same.

Most of the time she was real cheerful, though, and funny. One time I was in my favorite bar and Juanita came pushin' through the double doors and said, "Look, everybody, I got eggs about to hatch," and pulled these chicken eggs out of the top of her muumuu. After a coupla beers she said, "Well, I'd better go, I think they're hatchin' right now," and with another look down her muumuu, she got up and left. This particular bar was a great place for things like that to happen. During Rodeo Days people would ride their horses into the bar and nobody'd think twice about it. Juanita would also come into the bar with her rooster on her shoulder and set the place on its ear. If I were in there havin' a drink she'd point her finger at me and laugh, "Caught ya!"

You know, I was raised to be a lady and taught in a convent school that I was to stand back and keep my mouth shut. Well, I crossed the Golden Gate and met Juanita and finally opened my mouth. And if people didn't like it, that's too damn bad. Juanita helped me to be stronger, a little tougher, which was just fine in my book, honey!

BARELY DEAD CRAB CIOPPINO

Every Friday night would be crab cioppino night, come hell or high water. We'd get all these crates of green crabs wrigglin' around and tryin' to pinch ya if ya made the mistake of gettin' too close. A crab can pinch the daylights outta ya so if you're gonna make cioppino make sure there's nothin' wrong with your reflexes or somebody might find a pinkie in the stew. First I'd get my big crab pot boilin' and then I'd throw the suckers in, head first. When the crabs were dead but just barely cooked through, then you pull 'em out with tongs and throw 'em in a basket, one by one, until all your crabs is done for. You haveta have your crabs alive when you start 'cause if you start with a dead crab it could just turn the whole damn thing to poison. It's bad enough poisonin' your own family without killin' off a restaurant full of people.

I used to give terrycloth towels to my customers, one for their necks and one for their laps, and bowls of water to wash in, but they'd still come out a mess. We'd always save our #10 cans for cioppino night so everybody could throw their shells in 'em and this saved a little wear and tear. We'd also serve loaves of French bread to sop up the sauce and that's about it.

Anyway, after you got your crabs dead, then you chop up some green peppers and yellow onions and mess 'em around on the grill until they're sorta soft 'n glassy-lookin'. Throw on some chopped garlic and celery and mess 'em around with the onions and peppers. Throw that into your cioppino pot and add your canned tomatoes. Just plain tomatoes, nothin' fancy. Now you got all them Italian tomatoes and Mexican tomatoes and God alone knows what kinda other tomatoes, but all you put in, honey, is plain old American tomatoes with nothin' in the can but tomatoes. Put in some water, too, so you have somethin' to boil away.

Take your basil, but before you throw it in, rub it between your two hands to freshen it up and break up any bits that might tickle. Throw in whatever Vege-Sal you want. Let this sit there on a low fire for awhile, maybe an hour or maybe two hours or whatever time you have. I mean, you don't just mess spaghetti sauce together and dump it on your noodles, do you? No. Put in a couple bay leaves and a couple cloves and a few peppercorns and a lotta parsley at the end so it doesn't turn black and make people wonder what in the hell you've yanked outta your yard.

Now you tear apart your crabs and throw away the guts and mucky stuff and eyeballs and all and then crack 'em up and down and throw 'em in your pot. Throw in your shrimps and clams in their shells, too, and some sorta whitefish, doesn't matter. Muddle all this stuff together and let it all simmer real low until everything sorta falls apart. Remember to keep your fire down low so nothin' burns, just burps away by itself until you've got people around you whinin' for their dinner and makin' your life hell. I always used to say, "I love people, it's the public that's such a pain in the ass." Animals are a lot easier, mainly 'cause they can't talk.

I just love crab and so did Dick. Once Dick told me that what he'd wanted all his life was to eat his fill of crab and not have to stop because he was broke or had run outta crab. So I went crabbin' every day. I think we killed off half the crab population at the time. We had crab newburg and crab cocktails and crab louie's and crab cakes—crab in every form on this earth. At the end of all this, one day I forgot to take the old stinkin' fish bait I used for crab outta the car one crabbin' day and when poor Dick got home from a business trip and got into the car he thought we'd finally caught ourselves enough crab since the entire car smelled like low tide. Took awhile to remember the fish bait, which I'd left in the trunk, and by that time Dick decided he'd had his fill and didn't want to even SEE another crab for awhile.

SAUSALITO SPECIAL SALMON

I didn't make salmon all the time, just when it was the season and they didn't cost an arm and a leg. Also it was sorta finicky to fix but I'd get Marge to do it when I didn't feel up to it myself. When I did make it, what I'd do is, I'd put the water on to boil in a big enough pan to fit your salmon and the top of your stove, both. I'd throw into the water a couple handfuls of picklin' spice and lemons, cut up and squeezed. Then I'd take my nice fresh salmon and lay 'im out on a tea towel and tie each end so I could pick up each end of the towel with a fork to pull it outta the pan when it was done. This way you don't burn your hands all to hell. When your water is boilin' hot you lift your towel fulla salmon and drop 'im into the water, bring it back to the boil and then turn down your fire so your fish'll just simmer for ten or fifteen minutes, dependin' on your fish. Then you pull out the towel with your forks and sorta roll the fish off the towel onto a sheet pan, right away immediately or you're gonna have one sorry-lookin' fish. I always put lettuce leaves on the sheet pan first like a kinda bed so when you need to roll it over on its other side to peel the skin off, it's easy as one-two-three and it'll look bee-yoo-tiful. But you have to do it exactly the way I say to do it, puttin' it in a tea towel and rollin' it out onto lettuce leaves and move quick as you can or half your scales at LEAST are gonna come off and your salmon'll look like shit. Never forget to put a maraschino cherry in its eye and lemon wedges around it when you serve it, and parsley.

Never forget your parsley! Parsley looks good, like itty bitty trees, and is full of whatever it is that keeps your breath from smellin' fishy. If that don't bother you then skip the parsley.

CATHOLIC SOLE

This is real soul food since Catholics use to haveta eat fish on Fridays before the Pope let 'em off the hook. Let the fish off the hook too, if you catch my drift. For years and years and YEARS I made sole every Friday until Catholics could eat meat and that put the fried sole outta business. What I'd do is, I'd just fry it plain in butter, keepin' my fire medium so the fish didn't toughen up or fall apart. Frozen fish you'd have to do somethin' sneakier with, but mine was always fresh, just like the fishermen who caught it. Fresh and simple. If you felt like it you could put it in beaten up egg and then roll it in flour or bread crumbs and then fry it. The way I always understood it from my convent days is, people had to eat fish for the good of their souls and if it was a little on the plain side, that was probably better for 'em in the long run. A little lemon on the side and a buncha parsley and Mass the next mornin'— and all you have to be afraid of is sayin' somethin' shockin' to the preacher.

Vegetables

"Save Your Soul Sauerkraut"

ROBERT FRITSCHI:

Juanita and I were friends before I was her landlord in Glen Ellen, but once I did become her landlord it became a habit to eat three very large square meals a day at the so-called family table. If you ate there, it was free. However, quite often she requested that I eat in her quarters. She would consolidate the debris on her bed so there was a vacant corner. Juanita would then phone downstairs and order somebody to bring up dinner for me. So some poor waitress had to thread her way up the back stairs, carrying my prime rib, salad, side dishes and half a gallon of milk. If the poor girl did not get it right the first time Juanita would throw it at her. This embarrassed me no end because I was quite capable of rustling up my own grub, but I was not permitted. So I would sit at my corner of the bed and pack it in. Eventually I became worried that I was going to end up looking like her if I kept up eating that way—300 pounds of cholesterol.

Juanita had a thing about feeding the world—at her expense. If you were a paying customer she saw that you ate more than you paid for. If you could not load enough food onto your plate all by yourself from the buffet-style service, then Juanita would circulate around the dining room with a platter of food. "Oh, honey, you're not eating enough. You're going to waste away." So saying she would deposit a slab of meat or a batch of chicken on some patron's plate.

If this was not enough, I think that all the hippies and riff-raff had put some sort of a mark on her door. They came from far and near with their tales of woe and she would feed them, saying they could work it off. They got the food but Juanita did not get the work, as work was alien to that class of people, I guess. What always amazed me was that the matrons shouldered their way to the buffet table seemingly oblivious of this constant fringe of potheads. The food that was not consumed by this array of people was carried off by the kitchen help, which had very sticky fingers. The only time they worked hard was when they were carting off a ham, a slab of meat or a case of canned goods.

Juanita was always telling other people to throw food out too, if she was mad or something didn't look quite right. Without a thought she'd throw out a whole batch of something and ask someone to make a whole new batch. No sense of business at all. She used to spend 60% to 70% of her gross on groceries which is an absolute no-no in the restaurant business, where one should spend no more than 30% at most. A lot of food spoiled before it ever got cooked, too. Sometimes the refrigeration would be broken and whole bunches of chickens, for instance, would have to be deep-sixed along with whatever had been forgotten and was walking around in the back of the refrigerator.

Stealing was a major problem, though. Since Juanita had no inventory control, she never knew what she had or what had already been stolen. She would open up the reefer to find the gallon of mayonnaise or the wheel of blue cheese for her salad dressing was gone. Every night prime rib would walk out or a ham would disappear out a back window and she wouldn't realize it most of the time and wouldn't do anything about it if she did notice. She kept complaining that she wasn't getting all the money she should be getting for the food she had sold. Turned out, waitresses were cheating her by double-ticketing. A couple of us volunteered to collect the monies as each sale was made and the receipts for that first weekend were almost double. Every once in awhile we'd be sitting there collecting the money into paper bags and at a high sign from her we would go outside. When we were told it was safe to come back in, back we'd come, avoiding the sheriff who had dropped by to collect some judgement against her. He'd find a restaurant full of people and ten dollars in the till.

Of course, employees didn't have it all that easy. The ones that didn't have hard heads and ear plugs didn't last more than their first shift. Juanita assumed that everybody knew how to do things the "Juanita way." She was, however, oblivious to the fact that she always forgot to instruct the employee about anything. So when an offending employee did something Juanita considered wrong, they could only stand there in bewilderment while being reduced to a thin spot on the floor. You'd find them hunkered down sometimes behind the dishwasher cowering under a hailstorm of crockery. As a result of this, Juanita had to do without competent help a lot of the time, having driven off all the good ones, ending up stuck with the ones who did not care about anything and endured her frequent tirades as if they were one of life's minor inconveniences. They often weren't all there mentally, anyway, and were usually given to drink. Some would have just enough brainpower to figure out how to work for Juanita and were immune to her screaming and the objects she'd lob at them. An exception was Joe Foley, an old friend of hers, a nice guy. He was sort of like her maitre d'. I never could understand why he never set himself on fire. He'd sit in the lobby in his coveralls smoking these stogies and since he never had an ashtray he would simply flick the ashes into his breast pocket. I kept watching for him to go up in smoke, but he never did.

Of course Juanita set the tone for the place. I remember once I was at home, near the restaurant, working in my garage. A dump truck rumbled up and deposited Juanita unceremoniously on the garage apron. She was quite drunk. Somehow I managed to wrestle her into a chair in the shop office where she slept it off. I tell you, I was always entertained by Juanita and at Juanita's. To eat at her place was never just the mundane act of feeding one's face; rather it was to live for awhile in a wacky, goofy, wonderful world in which it seemed that the hilarious and improbable lived side-by-side.

HOMETOWN HOMINY GRITS

There's a lotta energy for folks in grits. I can't say my sun rises with grits, but they stick to your ribs and that's a lot more than you can say for a lotta things. What you do is, you follow the directions on your box of grits and don't do anything fancy with 'em, like addin' cheese or hot chili peppers because that just isn't grits, honey, that's tamale pie. Then you pour your grits into a bakin' dish and let it set and next day cut it into squares and fry 'em in butter until they're brown and crunchy on one side. Don't fry 'em too long or it'll be just like eatin' shoe leather. A little milk gravy is good on grits and strawberry jam, too. Another good thing about grits is you can serve 'em with practically anything and get away with it.

SMASHED HASH BROWNS

You have to cook your potatoes first and make sure you put them in cold water and then boil 'em until they dent a little when you pinch 'em but aren't squishy. Then you peel off their skins with a spoon. A peeler is just so much wasted money and a spoon works a whole lot better. You try it and see. Then you grate the potatoes with a little hand grater or shove 'em through a ricer, whatever you like best and either way is okay with me. Plunk down a handful on your grill or hot skillet and smash 'em flat with your spatula and set a big hunk of butter on top.

Dick always wanted the cooks to use oil and I always insisted they use nothin' but butter since to my mind fryin' hash browns in oil is like puttin' catsup on a good steak. They'd haveta see which one of us was on duty to know what to put on the grill. Dick used to get kinda grumpy when they didn't use oil but I tell you, if I tasted hash browns done with oil there was hell to pay and no mistake!

The butter melts as the first side cooks and it runs into all the potatoes and when it's time to turn 'em over, the second side is already greased up good and with no extra effort on your part. If you make the mistake of puttin' the butter on your grill first it will turn brown too soon to do the potatoes any good and my way takes care of that. Don't be a miser with the butter and don't forget to smash 'em with your spatula first. Good way to make hash browns and get even with your enemies, both.

SHREDDED ZUCCHINI

This was what we always served with hash browns and steak. It's easy and cheap and you can't help but grow a hell of a lot of it in summer since you can grow zucchini on the moon. It's good for you, too, anything that's shaped like that is good for you, like cucumbers and carrots and suchlike. Well, anyway, zucchini. You scrape it and shred it and put it in a skillet with melted butter and sprinkle on your Vege-Sal and there you are. No wear or tear.

OKIE FRIED POTATOES

When I was in business in Sausalito, this was before I dried myself out, cops arrested me and put me in jail six times in one year for bein' drunk 'n disorderly. They were one hundred percent right all six times since I was about one hundred percent drunk and one hundred and fifty percent disorderly. Some days I couldn't hardly raise my head so generally I slept in my car out in the parkin' lot or lay down on the illegal couch I kept in the restaurant with a pile of newspapers for a pillow and when a customer would come in I'd tell 'em to make their own breakfast since I was just too plain tuckered out from partyin' Some days I'd manage to get on my feet but still feel evil and cross lookin' at all the potatoes I had to turn into hash browns, so what I'd do is, I'd make Okie Fried potatoes. You wash your potatoes and throw 'em in a pot of cold water and then boil 'em 'til you can fork 'em. If ya got the energy, peel off their skins with a spoon, then cut 'em up any which way and then fry 'em in butter and oil and sprinkle on your Vege-Sal. This is less of a headache on those days when you have headache enough yourself and though people would be kinda disappointed not to get my hash browns they didn't say nothin' to me about it since I didn't look like any friggin' Betty Crocker, honey.

VERY MASHED POTATOES
With All Around Good Gravy

The thing about mashed potatoes is you have to mash 'em and mash 'em some more. They're not called Sorta Mashed potatoes are they? No. So what you do first is, you peel your potatoes and cut 'em up into quarters and throw 'em in a pot of cold water. Bring your potatoes to a boil and boil 'em until you can fork 'em. You can use the water maybe later so don't go throwin' it away. Just drain your potatoes and then mash 'em. If you want to you can put 'em through a ricer and they'll look like little worms but you can mash 'em afterwards and nobody'll know the difference. Kids would rather they looked like worms, anyway, but then they'd probably play with 'em and there isn't much in this world makes me madder than people playin' with their food. Mash 'em until they're real fluffy and then add your warm milk or warm potato water. Don't ever never add your liquid before all your lumps are gone and don't ever never put in your liquids cold or there'll be hell to pay.

Now about the gravy. When I cooked my first meal for Dick I made thick lumpy potatoes he called "potato poultice." He said my gravy was so thick he could cut it with a knife and that it tasted like wallpaper paste and I cried because I'd used practically a whole can of good Crisco and didn't get nothin' for it but insults. I guess he sorta figured he'd gotten hoodwinked since I looked like the kinda woman who knew how to cook. But he didn't get mad, he just showed me how to make potatoes and gravy right, and the right way to is to mash the hell outta your potatoes and to take your butter and drippings from your meat if you have any and keep stirrin' it up over a low fire and add a little less flour than what you have in fat. Keep stirrin' it and whiskin' it and pullin' it off the fire so it won't get thick and lumpy. When it's thick enough, but not too thick, then you add your warm vegetable broth or milk to it, but it's gotta be warm or you'll have lumps. If it's beef gravy you're makin' you add beef broth, not milk. Never serve fried chicken without milk gravy or your family will feel like they've been robbed. Likewise, never serve milk gravy or beef gravy, either, with prime rib. With that you just use the juice and if you've done your prime rib right that'll be plenty. In case you think I've yakked on too long about this, think again. Gravy is somethin' people just can't forgive you for, like eggs done wrong. Once Dick criticized my gravy after we'd been married awhile but by then he shoulda known better than to get my goat that way and I threw the whole dinner table over.

BLACK-EYE PEAS

You buy yourself a bag of peas and then you wash 'em and check 'em out to make sure there aren't any rocks in 'em and then you wash the crap off 'em. If you don't do that someone could lose a tooth and it might be you. Put 'em in plenty of water but don't put in any salt or they'll stay just like rocks even if you boil 'em 'til doomsday. After your beans are soft is when you add your Vege-Sal. I never did put anything else in my black-eye peas because you have to think of your vegetarians on New Year's Day and that they can't have any of the good pork ribs or pickled herring, and if you throw salt pork into your black-eye peas then they're just gonna have to make do with sauerkraut. Sauerkraut's okay, but you're not gonna have a whole lotta friends visit you NEXT New Year's if you've only given 'em sauerkraut to face the new year with.

HACKED CABBAGE

You put oil and butter in a big iron skillet and melt it down and hot. Chop up your cabbage—you oughta do this before you heat up your butter or you'll have to pour your fat out and start all over again—and throw it in the skillet, stirrin' it 'round and 'round until it wilts. Turn the fire down now and let your cabbage get real nice and golden brown and after about twenty minutes or so you got fried cabbage to be proud of. Just add a little Vege-Sal and that's all there is to it. I used to like to walk around my restaurant dishin' this out to folks who looked like they needed it. I'd tell 'em, "Eat it or wear it, honey," and inside three seconds the cabbage was inside THEM.

HOT 'N CREAMY POTATOES

I used raw potatoes for this and gave my hands and the Bag Balm a rest. What I'd do is, I'd make a nice cream sauce outta butter and flour and milk and then slice up some plain brown potatoes and then cuddle 'em up together and there you are. You have to cook it first, though, in an oven set to maybe 350 degrees for just about an hour, dependin'. If you lose track of yourself and make too much sauce, then all you have to do is cut yourself up more potatoes. Likewise, if you have too many potatoes you can mix yourself up some more sauce. It's easier doin' things that way than worryin' yourself sick about cups a' this and cups a' that. Never could stand that finicky way of doin' things. You can peel your potatoes first if you don't mind losin' those vitamins and you can set little clumps of butter on the top to make it even better. If you want to get fancy you can sprinkle cheddar cheese on top or buttered crumbs. I don't care, whichever.

ROASTED ONIONS
AU NATUREL

Raw onions put me to sleep in about ten minutes. I eat a raw onion and, pow! I'm out like a light. I'm religious about eatin' onions since they keep all kindsa viruses away, especially when you eat onions AND garlic. That'll whip the sniffles by noon. But you can't be in the restaurant business and be sleepin' all the time so whenever I felt like I needed my onion fix I'd fry some up or roast 'em or boil cut-up onions in water and drink it down. My favorite way is roastin' 'em, however, and it's real easy to do.

Just set your regular yellow onions in the stove and bake 'em like potatoes, inside their skins. They get real dark and that's when they're done. You haul 'em out and cut 'em open and peel 'em and, boy, are they good! This is really the "no-tears" way to go for you kitchen crybabies. Good idea, too, if somebody's stolen your kitchen knives. That almost happened to me, once, but I caught the little weasel just as she was sneakin' out the door. I could let a prime rib or a ham walk out every once in awhile, but I sure as hell wasn't gonna let my knives disappear! You lose your good knives you might as well close up shop and go fishin'.

HOT HEAD CAULIFLOWER

First you pull a cauliflower apart into small but not too small pieces. Heat a pot fulla oil and when it's good and hot drop your cauliflower in and let it fry like hell. Scoop it out with some kinda slotted spoon and put it on paper towels and Vege-Sal it and it tastes just like popcorn, only better. You can also take your whole head and drop it in the pot, leavin' on some of your leaves and puttin' your head end down and your bottom end up, fryin' it good and brown before fryin' the other side. You can put it in a bowl and pour on some sorta cheese sauce or just Vege-Sal. This is a pretty way to do cauliflower but it can just play hell with your buffet since you're gonna get people yankin' at it and more chance than not pullin' the whole damn thing out onto the floor. People hack away at food like you wouldn't believe, whooeee! Once I almost had to smack some guy for sawin' away at a ham until I thought I'd lose my mind. It's not that they do it on purpose, they just act dumb on general principles.

NUTLESS WONDER RICE

I'd chop up a carrot real fine and sauté it off in some butter and then mix it up with steamed rice and add a little bit of soy sauce. You just can't imagine how good this is and people always think it's got nuts in it and some people think it has meat in it, like Chinese rice, but a vegetarian can eat it and not feel like they've stabbed a cow or somethin'. If you don't feel like goin' to even this little trouble you can just chop up your carrot and throw it into the rice without cookin' it first and you have to be a real expert to tell the difference. I've given this recipe to some famous people and they serve it to their fancy friends and nobody knows it's just plain carrots and rice, poor people food. It's good for you, too, but don't tell your kids that.

SAVE YOUR SOUL SAUERKRAUT

My mother put me in a convent once so I wouldn't give in to temptation on Main Street. I already had, sorta, but she didn't know that. I liked the convent but the Mother Superior was one tough cookie and when she caught me eatin' this bee-yoo-tiful peach I was supposed to be peelin' for preserves she slapped me silly and gave me the punishment of helpin' with the sauerkraut detail. I had to turn a crank on a machine that shredded cabbage, but nobody told me that outside there was this 2-ton truck loaded with heads of cabbages and that I was expected to shred it all! I cried, my arm hurt so much, but when I switched to my left arm I hit my elbow on the crank when my arm went around so I had to switch back to my right arm. It took me three days to get that friggin' cabbage done with only time off to eat and sleep. I decided then and there that I'd be a lot of things in this world when I grew up, but I'd never ever be a sauerkraut maker or a nun.

This is a nice recipe for sauerkraut but it's a hell of a lot easier just to buy a gallon of the stuff and say to hell with it. First you get some bad kid to shred twenty pounds of cabbages, only you have to take the creepy leaves off first. You have to get yourself a barrel or a stone crock but you better make sure you wash 'em before you put the cabbage in because you don't know where they've been. You'll need about a cup of pickling salt for what you're gonna have to do next, which is put in a layer of cabbage and then sprinkle salt on top and keep on goin' to almost the top and then stop. Take your potato masher or baseball bat or whatever and pound the cabbage down and then put another layer of salt on top of that. Then you have to put a breadboard or a plate or somethin' on the top to keep out any visitors and weight that down with a rock. Cover that with a clean rag and tie it with a piece of twine and there you are. After a couple a' days you'll see it bubblin' and if there's any scum you better skim it off and throw it to the pig, if you have one. Keep your crock in a cool place, no more than 55 degrees or you might ferment somethin' you don't even wanna THINK about. When the kraut stops bubblin', it's done and you have to figure out where to keep twenty pounds of kraut and good luck, honey, if you don't have a big refrigerator. You can put it in sterilized Ball jars but the idea of that makes me feel woozy so better just to give it to your friends or serve Pork Loins in Bed real often. Kraut is also good with pork chops like the ones we have in this book.

Breads

"Convent Mush"

BOB MACDONALDS:

The first time I went to Juanita's I just sort of sat there at the table until she saw me and yelled, "Don't just sit there! If you want something help yourself!" From then on whenever I wanted a beer I'd go get one. That's the way she did things, if she was too busy or there weren't any employees around.

One time sixteen of us went to her place and sat down at this big round table she had and when she caught sight of us she yelled, "You son of a bitches, you didn't call me! I don't have any food in here, so you can just all starve for all I care." Then she added, after a minute, "Well, maybe I can find you something after all," and went into the kitchen. She came back out some time later with a bucket of scrambled eggs and pounds of fried ham, the best I'd ever eaten, and English muffins to die for and lots of great strawberry jam. More food than you could imagine coming from a kitchen that didn't have any.

I'll never forget the time Juanita's cook showed up drunk. Boy, was she mad! I had these sorority girls with me that had just come in from Michigan and they were simply riveted by all the screaming and hairpulling going on. I guess he had messed up everything, mixing the hamburgers in with the eggs, or something, and Juanita just swiped it all off the grill and threw it in the garbage can. Then she started cooking all the orders herself and was cussing up a blue storm when she saw these two girls I'd brought with me. Suddenly she turned to them and yelled, "I don't usually talk like this, honey," and then went right back to her tirade just as if she hadn't said anything at all.

Maybe the funniest time was when I brought a couple of priests with me. We were sitting around visiting when Juanita came up to say hello and I introduced them to her. She said, "I'm gonna see you get a picture you'll never be able to show your parishioners," and she got me to take a picture of herself with a boob on each one of poor Father Ed's shoulders. He was just tickled pink about it.

PROPER ENGLISH MUFFINS
With Sinful Strawberry Jam

I was always real particular about my English muffins and only bought the kind they don't make anymore so you're outta luck. You can buy other kinds, though, or make your own if you've got nothin' better to do with your time. Whatever, make sure you cut 'em open with a fork, not a knife, because a knife squashes your muffins and I just can't stand that. In my kitchen anybody didn't fork a muffin proper was apt to get *themselves* forked, honey, and I mean it! Any time somebody came in that didn't have much to do but eat, I'd collar 'em and take 'em off to the kitchen and set 'em down to fork a few muffins, just to work up an appetite plus pick up a little skill along the way. I had actors and cops and all sorta politicians sittin' forkin' muffins and this one guy that just had hooks for hands, he could fork muffins faster'n anybody else. I was real proud of 'im. One time Lee Rae's Aunt and Uncle walked in after drivin' a long ways and I said to 'em, "You don't have time to eat right now, you have to fork me some muffins," which they did for about three hours, havin' a ball. Every time after that when they'd come over for dinner, first they'd come into the kitchen to do a batch of muffins. One Admiral used to come in fairly regular and though he was a little slow at first, he picked up speed as he went along. Forkin' muffins just don't come natural to some people and you have to be patient 'cause they can't help it if the Good Lord goofed. That Admiral got sorta proud about how good he got, so you see what you can make of some pretty poor merchandise.

Next thing you have to do is, you have to butter your muffins before you broil 'em so the tops'll be crunchy and the bottoms all buttery and the edges all kinda burned just right. Then you have to put lots of strawberry jam on 'em, lots 'n lots. I used Puritan Strawberry Preserves only you can't find that anymore, either, so maybe you better make your own. I hope you don't have a payin' job because if you're makin' muffins and jam all the damned time you'd better be rich or married to somebody's got money, otherwise, honey, you'll be eatin' your muffins 'n jam under some bridge somewhere and God knows where you'll find a stove. I'll tell ya how to make strawberry jam later on but now I'm thinkin' about English muffins and can't do everything at once.

I used to go through muffins like some women go through men but this recipe only makes about two dozen muffins if you're payin' attention to size. Mix up two cups of hot water and two cups of scalded milk and two tablespoons of sugar, 2 teaspoons of Vege-Sal and six tablespoons of butter and let the whole mess cool down to 125 degrees or where you can stick your pinkie in and it feels like you're takin' a bath. Add two packages of yeast you've already melted in four tablespoons of lukewarm water and throw it into your warm milk. Then you have to add eight cups of bread flour and stir it in good. Cover your bowl and let it rise in a warm place, but not where any chickens will find it since bread is catnip to chickens.

This takes about two hours and your dough will have slumped back into the bowl a little and look like you've done somethin' wrong but you prob'ly haven't if you've done everything I've told you to and not taken any shortcuts that always get you in trouble 'cause haste makes waste and no mistake. Grease yourself up twenty-four muffin rings if you've managed to find some store still sells muffin rings and I'm not sayin' you will, and fill 'em halfway up with your batter. Let your rings sit in a chicken-proof place 'til your dough has risen to the top of your rings, if you have 'em, and then put 'em on a hot, well-buttered griddle and cook 'em slowly 'til they're done, about fifteen minutes each side. You can test 'em with a straw if your broom is handy, otherwise use a toothpick. I know you've got toothpicks since you almost never see people pickin' at their teeth with their fingernails anymore, unless you're at home and too gassed to care what your family thinks. Your family'll be too busy forkin' your muffins to notice anyway and if they give ya a hard time don't let 'em eat any.

Now that we're finished with that, I'm gonna tell ya how to make Sinful Strawberry Jam. This is way WAY too good to be good for you, so eat a lot of it. First don't make this with crappy imported strawberries that've probably been picked when they're still green. Get yourself fresh straw-berries in the summertime and crush eight cups full. Add a cup of good local honey and half a cup of real maple syrup and bring 'em all to a boil in a saucepan. Lower your fire to medium high and cook your jam until there's only a third of it left. Add a squeeze of lemon, just to take the sweetness down a peg. Get yourself some tapioca flour, if you can find it, and add it to four tablespoons of water and add that to your jam. If you can't find yourself tapioca flour then just follow the directions on a package of good ole American pectin and don't cook your jam too long or it's gonna come out tastin' like you made it from berries trucked in from China. Put your jam in sterilized jars and make sure your lids suck on tight or you might be pushin' up strawberries from the other side.

Darrell Reed

FIFTY-CENT FLAPJACKS

If you're expectin' a recipe for my famous flapjacks you're gonna be disappointed since I always used instant from American Doughnut Company and I don't know where they went to but I think they're gone like my muffins. You can buy all kindsa doughnut mix but you have to buy it in twenty-five pound bags and unless your family likes flapjacks real well, you're gonna end up with a bag fulla weevils. You can use pancake mix but it won't be just the same. Anyway, you put the powder part in a bowl and pour your water in real careful, foldin' it in and not beatin' it. If ya feel like beatin' something, beat your eggs or find some jerk that needs a little civilizin'. Let your batter sit meditatin' for maybe fifteen minutes before you stir it down easy. This'll give ya lighter flapjacks and not those godawful hot clots of dough some people make, especially at those pancake breakfasts where it better be for a good cause since you're gonna get a bellyache for sure with those suckers hittin' bottom like rocks in a fishtank.

Wipe off your grill with a rag so your flapjacks won't stay permanently and then plop on your batter. I always used to dish out my batter with big old round soup spoons, not the dinky spoons you get nowdays. Put on your grill or your skillet as many flapjacks as you have room for since ya don't wanna be standin' there all day. When little bubbles rise up around your edges, don't wait 'til they all pop before you turn 'em over or you're gonna have yourself some pretty tough flapjacks, the kind I gave to the pig if I found someone makin' 'em that way. Once you got 'em turned over they should rise up straight like the sides of a hamburger. You can suit yourself about how big you want yours to be, but I'll tell you the truth, the first day I opened up for business my flapjacks were raw in the middle and I got tired of tellin' everybody to eat just the outsides and I'd make 'em more. That's how I started makin' my famous eeny-meeny ones 'cause it's just lots easier to cook through those than it is to cook through those great big hat-size ones most people make.

I always made special flapjacks for kids, especially if they were with their folks who were talkin' alot and had to be pacified before they started breakin' things. First you put down the eyes and smiley mouth and let those get brownish and then you put on the head and big ears for a rabbit and smaller ones for a dog and little bitty ones for a cat. Kids aren't too particular about the size of ears unless they're on their own head.

One time my husband, Dick, was just standin' around talkin' to these highway patrolmen at their table. I was busy mixin' up this big bowl of pancake batter and was tired and all of a sudden got mad that Dick had oughta be helpin' me instead of just jawin' away and ignorin' me, so I threw the bowl of batter at him. It hit the center post and splattered all over the patrolmen who didn't say anything at all, thinkin' maybe I'd do somethin' worse, so they just sat there quietly, pickin' the batter off their uniforms. Maybe they were afraid of what I'd throw next. Dick got the message, though, and went into the kitchen to mix up another bowl of batter while I cleaned it off the floor. We used to buy the mix in hundred pound bags and a good thing we did, too.

SQUASH BREAD

I like this bread a lot but I didn't make it myself, but that's okay 'cause I asked Micki how to do it. This is a good bread to make if it's the day after Halloween and ya don't know what to do with your pumpkin. Don't use the pumpkin you already cut up into a jack o'lantern 'cause your bread'll taste like your kitchen was on fire when you baked it. Plus there're gonna be bugs. Two Halloweens I wrapped 'round myself yards and YARDS of orange terrycloth and was a pumpkin and since I weighed over three hundred pounds at the time I made a real good one. Plus I was cookin' and with all that terrycloth I didn't need no towels since that's what I was, one big fat towel. I can't say I was the hit of the party since a lotta my customers came in drag and some of them were knock-outs. No way could ya tell they'd stuffed their bras with socks. One gal came as a crotch and danced on one of the tables, which I used to do before I got so e-n-o-r-m-o-u-s and had to stick to the floor.

You can use squash which is everywhere all year and tastes pretty much like pumpkin, or not so's you can tell the difference unless you use spaghetti squash and then your bread'll look like it's got worms. First you soak one and a half cup of raisins in hot sherry wine and drain 'em when they're all filled up like ticks. Then mix up six beaten eggs, one and a half cups salad oil, one cup cold water, three cups of mashed up pumpkin (or squash), five cups of flour, two and a half teaspoons of salt, three teaspoons of bakin' soda, four and a half cups of sugar, one teaspoon of cinnamon, one teaspoon of nutmeg and one half teaspoon of ground up cloves. Throw in your raisins. Micki says this'll make two large loaves and you bake 'em for one hour at 350 degrees. People always eat more of this than they think they should, but everything good in life makes you want more of it than you think you should. If life wasn't that way then we'd all be thin 'n real cranky.

CONVENT MUSH

I never will forget the dee-licious cereal we had almost every mornin' in the convent. It was a brown oatmeal mush and I've never had the like of it since, though I've looked. It was the same stuff people fed their calves and I guess since it made calves grow into cows the nuns thought it would do the same thing for us. It had oats and molasses in it and we had it every day we didn't have eggs, which was Sunday. What you might do is, you might mix up plain rolled oats and millet and coarse ground corn and things like that and then cook it in water and add milk and good old-fashioned blackstrap molasses at the end. You can get fancy and add raisins and chopped up dates and so on but it won't taste like what you'd get if you'd been put in a convent, like I was. The other thing I liked about the convent was the things I learned, like it was as much a sin to think a thing and not say it as it was to just say it. A nun told me that and ever after I've said everything I had on my mind because I don't wanna end up a sinner.

Sweets

"Micki's Secret Babycake"

JUANITA:

I was never much of a believer in sweets, maybe 'cause I'm so sweet already, ha ha. No, really, I think it's because I always drank so much Scotch that my sweet tooth got pickled. I remember when I was a child, I used to dearly love bacon grease mixed up with Karo Syrup and spread on a piece of white bread, and then sometimes in the summertime I'd get sent to all these different relatives, includin' an aunt and uncle who had this daughter named Maggie Crabtree. She was just a little snot and would make a cake and not let me lick the bowl. When I'd cry my Aunt Mag would make her mix up a whole new batch of batter and let me eat it all, if I wanted to. Sometimes I did and sometimes I didn't, dependin'. Since there hasn't in my life been better desserts than those, I usually don't have any at all unless somebody bakes me a birthday cake and then I'll have some of that. I always figured people oughta make their own dessert outta the fruit I had on my buffet and my wonderful blue cheese dressin' because nothin's better than that unless it's grease and Karo on white bread. Wouldn't have had a friggin' cookie on my buffet for nothin', honey, but I always kept after-dinner mints in a nice old urinal. That reminds me of those two marmosets I had once that became mintoholics. Just couldn't keep away from those after-dinner mints. That bartender I had, Everett, he just spoiled those monkeys in the mint department and no matter how I'd yell and yell he'd just give 'em some if they looked at 'im right.

Fruit, that's what people were supposed to eat at my place. Plus you had all those muffins and strawberry jam people were supposed to eat lots of all the time they was eatin' everything else. That way they had a little bit of dessert the whole time, if they wanted to. Sometimes I'd make apple pies for Sunday breakfast, if I felt like it, but I don't exactly have a recipe for apple pie since if ya can't make apple pie at your age, honey, it's prob'ly too late to learn.

There was this once I bought eight hundred dollars' worth of frozen yogurt, and to this day I can't remember why I'd do a thing like that. Filled up a whole fridge and not a one was ever sold to a customer. My help ate every damn one. I used to walk into my kitchen and there they'd be, sittin' around the table suckin' on all these things. They just kept on helpin' themselves until all eight hundred dollars' worth was gone. Saved me the trouble of advertisin' 'em to my customers, but didn't help my bank balance any.

Micki and Francesca used to make great cakes for me, sometimes, for my birthday or somebody else's or during the holidays when people wanted more'n just fruit. I remember when Micki, my bookkeeper, would hear our gardener's truck rollin' down the driveway. "There goes the meat!" she'd say. She'd get so upset knowin' I'd ordered another hundred dollars' worth of topsoil. The guy really liked good dirt and good dirt don't come cheap, let me tell YOU. His health went from bad to worse because he liked to eat 'n drink too much and was kinda fat and mostly grey around the gills. One day he looked REAL awful, so I had someone drive him over to the doctor. He was standin' in the waitin' room when he keeled over and died in the doctor's arms. He was only fifty at the time, which was sad sad sad. I was glad, though, that Micki had made 'im a real nice cake for his last birthday. It looked like a mound of dirt with a shovel stuck in it.

The best cake Micki ever made me was for my fifty-fifth birthday and it was this gigantic cake shaped like my hotel in Fetter's, complete with flags and little animals all around. That was the one I only let people eat the grass off and I kept the hotel part until it burnt up in the fire.

Anyway, I just let Micki and Francesca and Dr. Rashid give their own recipes since I think cakes are just too finicky for words, and they don't, or they wouldn't mess with 'em in the first place.

FRANCESCA BOWMAN:

One day this great big woman came into my nursery and asked me "What kinda flowers you got?" I gave her a bunch of marigolds and said she could have them and she invited me to come to her restaurant for breakfast next day and I did. It was wonderful. She kept on inviting me and so I ended up going there every day for seven years except when I was sick. Took my kids, too, sometimes. She gave me breakfast and sometimes lunch and dinner. I hated to go to any place other than Juanita's. She was such great fun to listen to and to be around. I helped a lot in the kitchen where it was just bedlam, with her shouting about people not working hard enough. Once I went in the kitchen and there was Juanita with spatulas in both hands beating this kid on top of the head. He took off and she took off right after him in hot pursuit. Usually she could outrun anybody else but I think he got away that time.

Somewhere along the way I started baking cakes for Juanita. They were my way of sayin' thank you. One night I invented mincemeat cake during an attack of insomnia. See, I always cook when I have nothin' else to do and so I was just sittin' there that night with this recipe for a brunch cake made with pineapple, only I didn't have any pineapple. So I went to the pantry and found this jar of mincemeat left over from Christmas and figured, "What the heck?" It turned out perfectly and I took it over to Juanita's in the morning and she and her mother thought it was so good that they asked me to make it any time for them and always gave me the brandy to pour over it. Got to where I could bake mincemeat cakes so fast it'd make your head spin. I could bake five or six in Juanita's oven and once I baked forty cakes in a month. Sometimes I'd bake for two or three nights at a stretch, baking like a crazy woman. I won Grand Prize for it once in a newspaper contest but this is the first time I've ever admitted how it was I came to invent it. My kids hate it for some reason. Go figure.

HOLIDAY MINCEMEAT CAKE

3 oz cream cheese, room temperature
1 cup sugar
2 tsp vanilla
1 egg
2 cups sifted flour
1 tsp baking soda
1 tsp salt
1/2 cup dairy sour cream
2 Tbsp slivered almonds
1 lb- 4 oz good mincemeat
2 Tbsp brandy

Grease a 9" tube pan or spring form tube pan or large spinach mold. Sprinkle bottom with the slivered almonds. Drain the mincemeat and reserve 1/2 cup of it for top glaze. Cream the cheese thoroughly till soft. Beat in the sugar and vanilla; blend in well. Blend in egg thoroughly. Add the flour, resifted with soda and salt. Add alternately with the sour cream. Stir in the mincemeat. Turn into prepared pan and bake 45-50 minutes in 350° oven. Cool on wire rack 10 minutes, turn out while still warm. Spread glaze on top.

Glaze: 1/2 cup mincemeat, 1 Tbsp. softened butter. Enough powdered sugar to make spreadable; add brandy to desired consistency.

Cake can be pierced with cake tester or fork while warm and some brandy (approx. 1/2 cup) may be drizzled into cake before it is glazed.

MICKI SMIRCICH:

Working in Juanita's, like I did, was sort of a cross between a circus and a nightmare, but it was great fun. Bakin' cakes was great fun, too, and I liked to make special ones for birthdays, especially for Juanita's. My hotel cake was white and my dirt cake was chocolate, so you can take your choice which one you want to do and make it any way you want. Once I made a flowerpot cake with my grandson, Cory. We baked it in a nice clean flowerport and then dumped it out when it was done. That was as easy as the hotel cake was hard, in terms of decoratin'. I buy whatever cake mix is cheapest, generally, but then I add something to it and to the icing which makes both taste better. You can buy the stuff at cake supply stores, one bottle for the cake and one for the icing, kind of a secret ingredient unless you do a lot of decoratin', which I do. They're called flavoring extracts and come in all kinds of flavors, take your pick.

The only nerve-wracking part about bakin' cakes—and I don't know if your house is like mine—is that my cats and dogs love cake. One night I went to bed with three cakes sitting on the table for when I was goin' to ice them the next day, but in the night my labrador ate them. I've learned to hide my cakes from the cats, too, since I've seen a whole day's work go down the drain when the cats are around. Usually I cut off all the uneven parts and give them to my cats and dogs, and to my son-in-law, too, just so they won't feel left out. Everything else about makin' cakes is easy.

MICKI'S DIRT CAKE

This is my chocolate cake but I decorated it for a gardener who used to spend all Juanita's money on dirt. First I bought the cheapest chocolate cake mix I could find and mixed it up according to what the box said and then put in some butter vanilla extract I got at the cake supply store. Then I made my icing, like the kind on the hotel cake, only I added some melted semi-sweet chocolate squares to it. You can add as much as you want, depending on how chocolately you want it to end up being. I made one round cake and one smaller round cake and then iced them in between and put one on top of another and iced that all over and stuck a shovel in it. It wasn't too hard a cake to make but I wasn't feelin' all that ambitious, considering everything.

MICKI'S WHITE HOTEL CAKE

This was a real challenge, I tell you! First I made sheet cakes out of white cake mix and added the butter extract flavoring I got at my cake supply store. I cut it up into all the shapes I needed and then glued them together with icing. You can make your cake up to a week ahead of time but you have to thin your icing down a little and then coat your cake with it so it's airtight in the refrigerator and also when you finally get to icing it you won't have crumbs all over the place. I always make a big batch of icing at one time in a bucket because it keeps in your refrigerator a long time and whenever I want some I can just scoop it out and there I am. Here's the recipe:

3 cups Crisco

6 tsp meringue powder

4 Tblsp warm water

2 boxes powdered sugar

Beat the above ingredients well and then add four more tablespoons warm water and two more boxes of powdered sugar. Doin' it this way mixes up better than putting it all in your bowl in the same time and ending up with lumps. Now add two teaspoons of almond extract and two teaspoons of vanilla. If you want another flavoring, like butter vanilla, you can add that when you want to and any food coloring to the icing, too, if you're doin' something fancy. Beat it up good for ten minutes.

When I got all that done I made a hotel, gluing the parts together with icing, and grass all around it and animals all around on the grass and on the front porch. It was really a lovely cake but I don't have any good photos of it.

MICKI'S SECRET BABYCAKE

Some of my friends thought this cake was so good that they wanted me to enter it in a newspaper contest. But I always wanted to sort of keep it MY cake. At least until now, anyway. It's a different sort of recipe and makes a very good cake, believe you me, even if it looks a little funny to be buying baby food when you're eighty years old.

3 eggs, beaten
1-1/4 cups salad oil
2 cups sugar
1 tsp cinnamon
1 tsp salt
2 cups flour
1 tsp soda
3 small baby food jars: 1 apricot, 1 carrot, 1 applesauce

Mix liquid things and spices together. Mix dry stuff together and add 'em to your liquids. Mix well. Bake in 9" x 13" pan at 350 degrees for 30 minutes. Cool then frost with what's coming next:

1 quarter pound butter
1-8 oz cream cheese
1 pound powdered sugar
1 tsp vanilla

Beat your icing together and spread on your Babycake.

Darrell Reed

DR. PHILIP RASHID:

DESPERATION BREAD PUDDING

I tell you, I nearly lost my mind the night I showed up at Juanita's only to find Juanita alone, the place a mess and hardly a bone to cook with. I told her to go clean off tables while I did what I could with what I could scrape up in the kitchen. First of all, there was lots of bread. Lots and lots of leftover bread, probably because she didn't have many chickens to feed by then and kept on baking bread as if she did. I madly tore all that bread into chunks and poured two gallons of milk over it and some beaten-up eggs and then I mixed in brown sugar, a little salt and cinnamon and nutmeg, all to taste. Then I threw in some raisins and a handful of nuts, just for good measure and because Juanita happened to have nuts. Then I slathered lots of butter on top and threw that big panful in to bake in Juanita's pizza oven for dessert. After that, Juanita always made bread pudding out of her leftover bread because that first night people just gobbled it down. Gobbled it down like little pigs! It's very delicious, really, especially when you can't think of anything else to serve but simply have to have SOMETHING for dessert. The only tricky part is not to get it too soggy or too dry, but if you get it too soggy you can just throw in more bread and if it seems too dry you can just pour in some more milk. If you can't handle that then you'd better stick to toast and jam or go buy something at a nice bakery.

Galley Holidays,
Family Parties,
& Other Dangerous Events

"NEW YEAR'S ALL DAY DINNER
FOR GOOD LUCK ALL YEAR"

GALLEY HOLIDAYS, FAMILY PARTIES, & OTHER DANGEROUS EVENTS

I just love all holidays, but Easter's best. Always at Easter we'd have the buffet, like always, but also egg hunts in the dinin' room and out in the yard and baby chicks and bunnies, too, so kids could have a good time while their folks yakked at the table. Baby bunnies generally don't bite and the only trouble with chicks is sometimes kids squash 'em if you don't keep your eyes peeled. I always had ham and chicken, both, 'cause some people can't eat one or the other and some people are just too damn finicky for either one. I'm not countin' vegetarians 'cause they can't help it.

EASTER BRUNCH MENU

The Devil Made Me Do It Stuffed Eggs

Head of Ham

Fairweather Chicken

Hot 'n Creamy Potatoes

Hacked Cabbage

Thanksgivin' is the best time for big eatin' since nobody can usually remember what it's all about except for the roast turkey. One year the *San Francisco Examiner* came to the Galley and took a picture of my turkey steppin' out of the oven and they put it on the front page. Hope nobody got the wrong idea since there's no way you could roast a turkey like that, what with the feathers and all. We always had our usual buffet but also sweet potatoes I cooked and didn't get out of a can. Boil 'em until you can fork 'em, then peel 'em and mash 'em and put marshmallows on top and broil that until your top's brown and crunchy. Keep your eyes on the kids or they'll eat off all the marshmallows and it'll look like the cat's been into it.

THANKSGIVING MENU
Nameless Roast Turkey with Sageless Stuffing
Roasted Onions Au Naturel
Very Mashed Potatoes with All Around Good Gravy
Carrot and Soused Raisin Salad
Pickled Whatever

On Christmas we had our buffet, only a little more of everything and also dessert since people tend to think if ya don't eat sweets it can't be Christmas. We'd have our tree all set up with cookie ornaments all over it—unless somebody'd got drunk and ate 'em. Everybody always had a good time at the Galley on Christmas 'cause we were just like one big family, food served complete with argument. Everybody got a present, too, if I didn't run out of 'em, and we just had fun generally. I remember once I cooked a big Christmas dinner for my husband and mother-in-law and we sat there at that big table in front of all that food and I just got disgusted and said, "I'll never do this again. If I'm makin' a big friggin' dinner, I'm gonna share it," and so I did, and so I will until I'm stuffed forever in a urn.

CHRISTMAS DINNER MENU
Juanita's World Famous Prime Rib
Polk Street Salad
with Million Dollar Blue Cheese Dressing
Pickled Chicken Innards
Shredded Zucchini
Francesca's Holiday Mincemeat Cake

I always have my New Year's All Day Dinner for Good Luck All Year and I always serve the same things so if you don't like 'em once you won't like 'em any better the second time. I have pickled herring, because fish move ahead, and pork ribs because pigs root ahead and black-eye peas. I can't remember why black-eye peas, 'cause they don't do any gettin' ahead, they just lie there, but then so does sauerkraut and that's another thing you have to serve people if they're not gonna run into an almighty rotten string of lousy luck. Maybe the black-eye peas cleans up your air and eliminates odors, if you catch my drift, and sauerkraut gives you the trots and cleans you out. Like spring cleanin'. Everything to get you ahead in the new year, honey.

NEW YEAR'S ALL DAY DINNER FOR GOOD LUCK ALL YEAR

(see above)

BIRTHDAY SUPPER FOR SOMEONE SPECIAL

Great Depression Bean Soup

Kick-in-the-Kidney Salad

Adam's Downfall Barbecue Ribs

Smashed Hash Browns

Nutless Wonder Rice

Dirt Cake

Right after my second place burnt down—and I mean RIGHT after—I was supposed to cater this big tailgate breakfast at the racetrack nearby. I didn't have one second to think about the fire 'cause three days after I served up a sit-down dinner for three hundred and a tailgate breakfast next mornin'. I had to do all this cookin' at the Veterans' Memorial Building since my kitchen was kaput and cart everything around in pickup trucks. That mornin' I took over my big bathtub for the wine and all these chaferin' dishes and served up french toast and baked bacon and fruit salad and English muffins for maybe a thousand and everybody ate a whole lot and then started drivin' like crazy round and round so I was glad I'd given 'em enough to eat and even gladder they waited to race around until they'd finished eatin' since you wouldn't of believed the dust.

FAST TRACK TAILGATE BREAKFAST

Addled Eggs

Baked Bacon

Hometown Hominy Grits

Ham it up Salad

Proper English Muffins with Sinful Strawberry Jam

Once I hired these guys to do a luau and I bought four whole pigs. It was somebody else's idea but it seemed like a good one to me since I'd already had a luau in Sausalito when these Hawaiians buried a pig in my parkin' lot. Problem was, these people whose idea it was never showed up 'cause they'd gotten so drunk they forgot all about it. Anyways, I got all the stuff you needed to roll the pigs in only not banana leaves since all our bananas come naked. But somebody said, "Why doncha use cannon lily leaves, instead? They look a helluva lot like banana leaves and won't kill ya, either." So I went on up to Bob Fritschi's house and just stripped his poor plants bare. By this time we'd dug a big hole down in the rose garden and we put in wood and then we got rocks outta the stream and got 'em hot in a barbecue and dropped 'em in the hole.

What I did next was, I took my chicken wire and put gunny sacks on top of that and the leaves on top of the sacks and the biggest pig on top of that and then rolled the wire up around him like a cage and dropped the pig into the hole and dropped in more hot rocks and wood and then threw dirt on top. I had not even the littlest idea how to cook the damned pig and had to do it by gosh and by gum and somebody said it came out raw but they're lyin' 'cause that pig just fell right off the bone. I mean, I cooked the hell out of it for a whole day and ANYTHING'S gonna fall apart after that. Anyway, it was dee-licious! The other three pigs I stuffed into my ovens, head and feet and squiggly tails and all. They came out fine, too, but whooeee! did we have pig runnin' out our ears! We ate pig for days and days and DAYS.

HAWAIIAN LUAU GALLEY STYLE
Roast Suckling Pig or Head of Ham
Yank My Doodle (It's a Dandy!) Macaroni Salad
Sausalito Special Salmon
Hot Head Cauliflower
Squash Bread
with Sinful Strawberry Jam

Two things I gotta say last. One thing is, I always liked my dinin' rooms elegant and my caterin' parties, too. That's why I used all kinda bathtubs and old chamberpots and urinals and brass spittoons and so on. If you don't have any nice old things like that, don't worry 'cause you can think of somethin' just as nice. You can serve your buffet in a life raft or a canoe—I did that once and it was just loverly—or you can use just usual dishes if you aren't old enough to have gone to all the yard sales 'n thrift shops you have to go to to find enough good stuff. Don't give up, honey, with a little time you can do things right.

Second thing is, animals need to have holidays, too. Ya have to think of how hard it is on 'em all the time, puttin' up with assholes like us. I like to serve up kibble and canned food on different plates so all my cats in the house can have their own place to eat and not haveta worry about bein' jumped on right in the middle of dinner. Just think how much YOU'D like that every damn day. Then I give 'em scraps of hamburger or pork chop or anything I have left from breakfast. Put your bowls at all different heights so your young ones can eat up on the windowsill and your old ones can eat down closer to the floor. Now my friend Hughie, he used to go just overboard for his two old dogs and would line up a whole row of stuff. He'd have a bowlful of sausages and one fulla cheese and another fulla fried chicken and oreo cookies. Hughie's just not comfortable with himself if they don't have everything they might feel like eatin'. I tried to stop him since those dogs just got fatter and fatter and fatter and prob'ly would've exploded except they lost most of their teeth. I finally did manage to persuade him to only put out one or maybe two bowls for each dog but I know he still sneaks things into 'em, like cheese curls. Now those dogs are so old it isn't such a bad idea anymore, except for maybe a few maggots. I guess he still remembers that time years before when he was caretakin' a ranch and ran outta food and had to feed those animals everything he could lay his hands on. They were all saved in the nick of time or everybody would've starved to death, includin' Hughie, unless the cats got to 'im first and then they'd do okay.

Juanita's Photo Album

Isn't this just the most dis-gusted face you ever saw? Prob'ly somebody didn't show up for work and maybe I was a little hungover, too. And will ya look at that dirty muumuu! Whoooeee! Sometimes I didn't have time to change so I'd just turn 'em around so the dirty part'd be in the back. Or I'd keep throwin' clean muumuus over the dirty ones 'til by the end of the day I'd look like there was three of me. Outta sight, outta mind. This reminds me of that first day I opened up for business about 2:30 a.m. and some fishermen came in. "I want coffee! Gimme coffee!" They kept whinin' at me until I got so damn flusterated I just yelled, "Oh, pour your OWN damned coffee!" That's how that policy started, "Pour your own coffee, sugar's on the table and look for the cream." Saved a lotta wear and tear on the help. People got legs for a reason.

Here's my precious Sissy lookin' out the window!
Prob'ly for the Health Department since I seem to be
scrubbin' everything down real good. I always wore
my gold, high-heeled wedgies so I'd feel dressed up
even when my muumuu was dirty. It's mighty hard to
look sexy all day long, especially when you don't
hardly have time to brush your hair. You just don't
know what pigs some people can be sometimes. One
time these kids were in the kitchen throwin' eggs at
each other from this big egg basket I had. I grabbed
me some eggs, too, and threw 'em at the kids and
they were duckin' and yellin' and sayin' "Hey! How
come you're doin' this, Juanita?" I said, "I'm payin' for
these eggs so I might as well have the satisfaction of
throwin' some of 'em." When all the eggs was
throwed, I told 'em to clean up and I left, leavin' 'em
standin' there all hangdog, walls covered top to tit in
goop. Served 'em right, treatin' eggs that way.

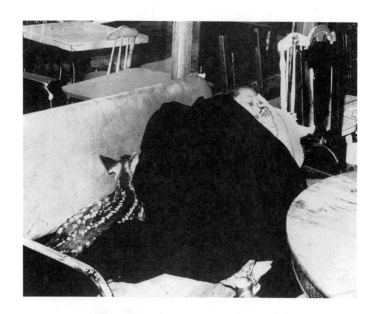

Oh, my precious, precious Sissy! We weren't supposed to have a couch in the restaurant 'cause those damnfool Health Regulation people thought you'd sleep on it. I used to pile newpapers at one end and then when I was tired I'd push 'em over sideways to make a nice sorta pillow. Then Sissy and I would go to sleep and let everybody just fend for themselves. Couldn't work 24 hours a day, and the deer couldn't either, so I got to where I could sleep anywhere and anytime. People would come in that I knew well enough to say, "Go scramble your own friggin' eggs," 'cause I was just too hungover and didn't wanna get up. Then I'd hear 'em just beat their eggs all limp-wristed and I'd yell out, "I've always taught you to beat your eggs better'n that!" And then they'd beat and beat and beat 'em and do a real good job. Sometimes, though, I'd have to get up and take the whisk away from 'em and do it myself.

This is another picture of my precious Sissy. She just loved beer, though I didn't generally give 'er any since two of us off the wagon would've been a mess, and I don't mean maybe. She liked my cookin' always, especially the flapjacks. We could eat a whole big plateful between us, and a buncha bacon, too. She liked hers real crisp. That deer would eat anything at all I'd eat, but that's the way you get if you grow up in a restaurant. You get so's you can eat just about anything that hits the table—or the floor, if you're a chicken.

Now this time clock, this was just the greatest idea I EVER had. See how proud I look? I was on my way to Reno and we pulled into this garage and there was this time clock on the wall. I asked 'em, "Hey, will you sell me that thing? Everybody's always tellin' me that they've waited for hours to eat and if I had a time clock like that I could prove which ones were dirty liars." So he let me have it for fifty dollars and I took the pendulum off and stuck it in my bra so he couldn't change his mind. Poor old clock burnt to death in El Verano and I never got another one for some reason. Maybe they was all burnt up by that time. Anyway, I had these order tickets made up and they were just like little lie detectors and if someone whined at me about how long they'd waited, I'd just pull their ticket out they'd punched in the time clock and point to the time and say, "Wanna change your tune, jerk?" and they generally would. I can't say things worked out smoothly after that, but smooth enough.

Juanita's
GALLEY
GATE 5 ROAD·MARINSHIP·SAUSALITO, CALIFORNIA

HOUSE RULES

1. WRITE YOUR OWN ORDER. Be sure to put your name on order so we can find you.
2. POUR YOUR OWN COFFEE.
3. PUT CARD IN TIME CLOCK AND PUNCH. This is the only time you can punch me and I will not punch back.
4. HAND ORDER TO COOK. Our food always guaranteed - but not the disposition of the cook.

NAME:_____

ORDER:_____

CHECK HERE FOR SPECIAL SERVICE*

SLOW ☐ **DON'T CARE** ☐

DAMN BIG RUSH ☐

*Doesn't mean you will get what you ask for - But check any one that will make you feel better.

N⁰ 54488

We started the "Pay Now Eat Later" plan to take care of people who walked out on their bills or had got too drunk to remember if they'd paid me or not. Sometimes when the service was real, REAL slow, people'd complain that it was really "Pay Now Eat Never." Can't please all the people all the time and I used to tell 'em, "Look, I don't charge prices high enough to take bullshit."

See how clean all those jam jars and sugar jars are? I kept everything i-m-m-a-c-u-l-a-t-e, I tell you! See that glomeration of chairs, all different? Once I bought all the same kinda chairs and some boys came in and had a fight and broke most of 'em up like toothpicks and I was back at the very beginnin' and thinkin' to myself, "What the hell? Might as well everybody sit on milk crates." Once these boys came in and threw sugar all over the floor and squeezed mustard into the juke box. Well, they made the mistake of comin' back. I let 'em get just past the Coca-cola machine and then slapped 'em down into the booth they'd trashed earlier. They kept on tryin' to get out but I'd just slap 'em back. Their coffee cups were right behind me so I picked 'em up and poured their cold coffee all over 'em and then I said, "Oh, I almost forgot, you like sugar in your coffee," and I dumped the sugar jar all over their heads and even into their socks. Whoooeeee!

Sally Stanford and I was helpin' with this fundraiser
deal but Sally didn't want the people clutterin' up her
restaurant and I did so there was where we were.
Since this was a publicity photo I thought the turkey
oughta be in on the deal, so there we are, me with my
turkey and my uplift and Sally with her uplift and her
diamonds. I had a lot more uplift, as you can see for
yourself, and I always did prefer turkeys to diamonds,
anyway, and hated mink coats with a passion.
Diamonds're just rocks, and mink coats mean some
poor minks are runnin' around naked, while turkeys
lay eggs and add to the atmosphere.

Can you believe I hauled this ferryboat in to shore in Sausalito? Practically had the tow rope in my teeth. Everybody thought it was sunk but a friend told me just the petcocks were open and the bilge filled up. I got permission to open 'er up as a restaurant just so long's I didn't dump the crap in the bay. We got her cleaned up and more or less on an even keel with old refrigerators 'n stoves 'n phone booths for ballast. Lotsa kids on the lam would sleep up on the top deck and if they did some work for me I'd feed 'em for free, only sometimes I'd feed 'em anyway. They were a pain in the ass, sometimes, but I always figured "growin' pains." Seems like a lotta bad luck happened there, though, what with the bike gang smashin' up the place and that IRS. When I left, some morons cut a door in the bilge durin' low tide and when the tide came in, it sank. Then it fell apart in the mud 'til nothin' whatsoever was left but its wheel.

I like this one of Rommell. He was so cute. Sally Stanford gave 'im to me. See, I went up to El Verano to fix up this place she said I could rent and I worked my tail off only to find out it'd been condemned. When I faced her with it, she said, "If anyone could get away with it, you could," and I was so mad I wouldn't speak to her for a year and a half. One day she sends me this fox and I never could figure out if she sent 'im to me 'cause she thought he'd bite me, or whatever. He used to run away every chance he got so we had to advertise for people to keep a lookout. Finally he ran away and the damnfool people what found 'im kept washin' 'im for some reason and he died. Don't have any use for those kinda people at all.

This is the Easter basket I made one year outta the hotel fountain that I'd already turned into a duckpond before I built a bigger duckpond out back. I wrapped up the duckpond part and then tacked on the basket handles. The fountain part I filled up with that green plastic crap and Easter eggs for the kids. It was real pretty and the kids just loved it! That's the same fountain I turned into a salad bar, but that was after the fire and after some son of a bitch stole the top part for some reason that escapes me. Takes all kinds, I guess.

This is such a nice picture of my bee-yoo-tiful bed. My animals just loved that bed, too, 'cause they could all fit on it without catfights most of the time. Sometimes I had iguanas on that bed and sometimes monkeys 'n sometimes my cocks, but this guy in bed with me is Jeff Lee, a newspaper photographer there to shoot me that day and a great guy willin' to take a risk. This is just exactly how everything was arranged before the fire burnt it all up.

(Photo by Tim Tesconi.)

This is another real good picture of my bed, only I got this look in my eye that maybe I'm loungin' there givin' hell to somebody about somethin'. Marge used to always say that when I'd get that look in my eye you'd better run. Maybe that's not what's happenin', though. Maybe I'm just tired and some reporter's askin' me too many damnfool questions. Sometimes I don't have the patience I have other times. Don't you just love those butterfly sleeves? They have a lotta give. Sleeves like that, you can make your potato salad or whack somebody upside the head and your arm won't give way. That bed was a bishop's bed from Monterey I bought from this guy who was usin' it as a sawhorse 'cause he made the mistake of buyin' it for his wife before findin' out if she wanted to sleep somewhere else. You can sure tell I was three hundred pounds there, cancha? Whoooeee!

This is one of Micki's birthday cakes she made me. Wherever she got that friggin' doll I'll never know. That was a real nice cake and they stuck money in my head but the best one of all was the hotel cake she made for my 55th birthday. That was just bee-yoo-tiful! The hotel was all surrounded by animals and grass. I let everybody eat the part of the cake with the grass growin' on it but I wouldn't let nobody touch the hotel part. I kept that and kept that until it burnt up.

This is the dirt cake Micki made for the guy we had workin' in the yard. She thought he oughta have a dirt cake 'cause dirt was what he was always dumpin' off on us since sometimes I liked to buy dirt instead of payin' the food bill. I also have this weakness for yard sales. Good dirt 'n yard sales are my downfall. Some days we'd have to just cook what we had and then wait until we'd collected some money and send somebody to the store for a chicken or somethin' to cook and just go along like that all day. Micki wasn't too happy about that since she was the bookkeeper. It wasn't real dirt, though, it was chocolate, and the guy just loved it even though he died not too long after.

This is me and that nice Doctor Francine Bradley. She always had her birthday at the Galley. We were always good friends 'cause she loved chickens maybe even more'n I did. She gave me some of my favorite cocks and would come whenever I asked her to if I had a sick chicken and gin wasn't doin' the trick. I told her once, "Well, I guess if the chicken dies it'll be pre-marinated," only I was just kiddin' 'cause I never cooked anything I petted or slept with, even if it would've made good soup.

I had this itty bitty rooster that Herb Caen wrote was "the smallest cock Juanita ever had." Problem was, all the hens was too tall for 'im and they don't say "henpecked" for nothin'. So Francine Bradley went somewhere or other and found me a little hen and we decided to have a weddin'. This picture is where they said their "I do's" only we said it for 'em. They just sorta pecked at each other. They were man and wife for years and I think part of this was the real good start we gave 'em.

This is that good 'ole pig, Erica. She just loved to eat. She'd follow anybody had a scrap a' bread and pin him against the wall until he'd give it to her. First she lived on the porch at the hotel on the other side of the windows so customers could watch 'er, but those damnfool Health Regulation people made me move her pen into the yard. After the place burnt down and we moved to Glen Ellen, she'd push the fence over and run on downhill to Russ Kingman's house and eat his patio furniture. Later on we gave up chasin' her and she went to live in this little grove of redwoods. That pig had a mind of her own! Finally I sold her to some people who said they just wanted her to live happy on their farm, but I sorta looked suspicious at bacon for awhile, just the same.

Oh, I used to just love to play with a good cock! Here I am with one. I'd always tell girls in my restaurant, "If you treat a cock right it'll do whatever you want." This is just a medium-sized one, but I had smaller ones and bigger ones. Once I had a real real big one but my chickens got nervous so I had to give 'im away.

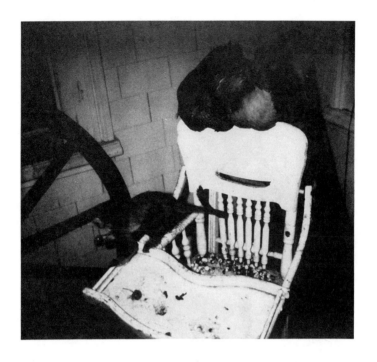

This is a picture of one of my little monkeys. He's eatin' himself an apple, looks like. Now Beauregard, he used to steal the maraschino cherries from drinks— sometimes he stole the drinks, too. One time he got into somebody's room and opened all the bottles in the bathroom cabinet and ate a whole damn bottle of Dexedrine. All night he was swingin' from the chandeliers, breakin' things as he flew around, knockin' over the vases of parsley on the tables. Wantin' a good stiff drink the whole time, I guess, but we made him go cold turkey. On the back of that high chair is two chickens sleepin' while that monkey is prob'ly up to no good. That's the best thing about a monkey—he just has no idea how to behave.

Here's me and my little jackass, Judge MacMahon.
Named 'im for a judge in the county I liked real well
who saved this baby's father from bein' given to the
guy who took 'im to the glue factory in the first place.
Rattleass was his name and there didn't seem to be a
fence could hold 'im. I used to climb all those hills
outside Port Costa and have to drag that jackass
home. Once I tried to sit in the trunk of a Camaro and
haul 'im along but he wouldn't cooperate. Guy had a
birthday and I brought Rattleass inside to sing Happy
Birthday to 'im. He was real touched, I can tell you.
Doesn't his mother there look surprised? No way
should she've got herself knocked up by a jackass, but
she did. Thank God that never happened to me.

Now isn't this sad sad sad? The hotel burnt down just about exactly one year after I made the fountain into a Easter basket. Up on that verandah was where I had my animals, thanks to the damnfool Health Regulation people. I saved all I could and then had to give in and climb down the ladder or go down with the ship and I couldn't do that 'cause I had other animals dependin' on me. People, too. We set up this old stove we saved off the porch and I cooked on that for a coupla weeks until we moved to Glen Ellen. Ribs, mostly, and chili. We got what we could from the ashes and then sat around, eatin' chili and watchin' this 'dozer squash about a thousand pincushion dolls into the muck.

I liked to put animals in my ads so customers could find me after I moved somewhere else. When I moved over to Glen Ellen some of my animals let themselves be caught but some just run wild in the bushes and got eaten by dogs. My peacock, Dominique, made it over okay, but my poor blind rooster didn't. Couldn't see where we'd went, I guess. One time I didn't leave the hotel property for nine months and you'd think stayin' put the way I did I wouldn't of spent much money, but I did. See, I had this tendency to spend other people's money somehow and the next book about me should be "How I Spent Everybody's Money." Either that or "How Not to Run a Restaurant." I wasn't long enough in Glen Ellen to do more than spend my *own* money, mostly.

This was when I was made an Honorary Member of
the American Association of those University
Women—a lot more fun than goin' to university, you
can bet your sweet ass. They came over for their party
to Port Costa the day I had my turkey in the bathtub.
What happened was, it used to walk the streets durin'
the day and sleep in this three-wheeled bike at night.
Only the bike had plastic around the sides and some
guy threw his cigarette in it and it caught fire. Poor old
turkey got scorched and I had to put it in my bathtub
and keep puttin' Bag Balm all over it, but when the
University Women got there I had to give 'em the
bathroom and 86 the turkey. I put it outside in a cage,
but it got pneumonia and I found it next mornin' all
crumpled over sideways. He'd been such a nice
turkey, too. He'd sit for hours lookin' at himself in the
hotel window, preenin' and preenin', and then he had
to go have his feathers burnt off. I shoulda put 'im
away but I got drunk and forgot. Lost a blind chicken
that way once. Didn't put him away and Hughie's dog
found him and killed him accidentally while he thought
they was havin' fun. I didn't find that out for years 'til
Hughie finally told me, after I'd mistakenly run over his
dog. What goes around comes around, only it took a
few years.

This is a picture of me lookin' evil and cross. I look like
I'm about to dump a bowl a' batter over somebody's
head, though my preferred method was to throw it at
'em. Actually what I used to do most of the time was
mix me up a big bowl of batter and then scoop some
of it out for flapjacks. If somebody chose that time to
bug me then I'd just sling the batter at 'em instead.
They'd just clean themselves off and act right—or I'd
do it again. Didn't usually take more'n once, though.
You see I'm dressed like I usually was, in a muumuu,
though I remember once cookin' all day in a bee-yoo-
tiful old nightgown and nightcap and once I dressed up
in a whole bolt of orange terrycloth and cooked all day
lookin' like a pumpkin.

Isn't this a bee-yoo-tiful picture? This was the fountain
outside the hotel in Fetter's. 'Bout the only thing was
left, too. Somebody stole the top part, but I took the
other two bowls along with me to Port Costa and
made it into a salad bar. Then the next place I went to
didn't need it so I turned it back into a fountain again,
and then when I moved next I turned it back into a
salad bar. Then there was that time it was an Easter
basket. I tell you, there just about wasn't anythin' that
fountain couldn't be turned into.

I liked to bake my own bread since people like to have a nice fresh loaf on their table and not just a lousy little basket a' crumbs. I bought the dough, then let it rise and then I baked it. Only this time they came out like tits. This picture was taken in the kitchen at Port Costa, but I had a stove right in the middle of the dinin' room in Winters so people could watch somethin' while they waited to eat. Kind of a floorshow. See how spotless my kitchen was? Vinegar 'n water is my secret for cleanin' everything so it'll smell like a salad and not like some funeral parlor.

Here I am givin' somebody a little hell. Maybe I didn't want my picture took or maybe I was hungover or somethin'. Never can tell. Sometimes I told people off 'cause they needed it and sometimes just on general principles, but you'll notice here that I'm not doin' anything much with my middle finger. If my middle finger got real involved, then, look out! Somebody was in REAL trouble.

This was that nice old bar at Port Costa. There I am, gassed to the tits, and I guess I'd decided to sleep instead of raise hell, but God help anybody who tried to wake me up once I was out. I'd come up swingin' and deck anybody not too quick on their feet. People always said I was like a war veteran, but the only wars I ever saw were the ones in my own restaurants. I guess I was thrown in jail a whole lotta times 'cause in one year I got sent up five times. One time this cop took me to the hospital and the doctor scratched my belly with pins and I didn't feel a thing. So they took me to jail since I was actin' near dead. Years ago I went to this dry-up farm after I hit Dick with a telephone one night. Just can't hit a man like that, unawares. Later on I was mostly on the wagon 'cept when I fell off. With a bang, honey, with a bang.

Here I am, servin' up too much food and never bein'
asked back. See my Vege-Sal? I used to carry a box
around in my purse if I was anywhere they didn't have
it. That's my burgundy beef and only one skillet to
cook it in, but I musta served up plenty 'cause all the
people there tryin' to sell food were outta luck with me
givin' mine away.

This was my salad bar in Port Costa. I always liked to put out things for people to look at, but somebody stole John Kennedy's head one night and never brought it back. I just loved that man, no matter what they say about him screwin' around. Maybe some doctor'd told 'im it was good for his back. It's good for everything else, unless you get caught by the wrong person, like his wife. See that great big box of minty picks? We'd go through minty picks like a pig through biscuits. I gave that bed tray to somebody who was sick and it's prob'ly in a dump somewhere now. Somebody stole that paintin' of me and if I ever get my hands on that broad that done it she'll wish she'd just had dinner and left it at that.

Here I am goin' to a party for Sally Stanford. I'm wearin' a lace tablecloth from Mexico and my Birkenstocks. Sally approved of everythin' but the Birkenstocks, but my feet were just charred to ashes, nearly, when my hotel burnt down and these shoes were just a godsend to my feet. Sally'd told me to comb my hair more often and when I told 'er I had just too many snarls she said, "mineral oil," so I did. But I couldn't get my hair to act right for her party so I just hacked it off with a razor blade. Did such a good job I'd hardly any hair left to put up. Usually I'd wear two or three combs in my hair—and sometimes up to ten, dependin'—but that night I had to glue that damned comb in to get it to stay put. I wore a tablecloth to Sally's funeral, too, not because we was in the restaurant business but because both times I'd run outta muumuus and money at the same time.

This was the end of the trail. Place was condemned and those damnfool Health Regulation people wanted all kindsa stuff done I had no money for. So Mother and I lived in the chicken coops and entertained ourselves feedin' the chickens. I found this big ole wheel out in the mud one day in Sausalito and I got ahold of it and dragged it in. Durin' the second fire, I found it blazin' away and rolled it downhill into the duckpond. It lost a few more spokes but I took it along with me until it fell apart entirely. I wish now I'd kept the hub. I'm sure I coulda done somethin' with it, put toothpicks in it, maybe. You can't see it in the picture 'cause it's gone by now. At least I'm not endin' up like the Cat Lady. She was this lady that decided one day that her house wasn't safe for her anymore so she moved out onto her front lawn with all her cats. We used to go by and take her cat food but she didn't live long. Sometimes my luck hasn't been too great, either, but at least I'm not gonna end up dyin' in a lawn chair by the sidewalk. Leastways, I hope not. I got way too much junk.

Photo by Garry Campbell

ABOUT THE AUTHOR/COLLABORATOR

Sally Hayton-Keeva is the author of (mostly) serious works of fiction and nonfiction, which this cookbook is not. This cookbook is an attempt by the author to prove to her mother that there is somebody in the world whose culinary inclinations are, at times, stranger than her daughter's. This is not so simple a thing to prove since the author once covered a birthday cake she made for her father with little silver candy balls, thus creating—however unwittingly—the world's first armored cake.

The author has long taken a back seat to her sister, fellow writer and cook, but she hopes this book will set matters straight and persuade her sister to forget all about the time the breakfast eggs exploded.

Hayton-Keeva lives near enough to Juanita to often enjoy her company, but beyond the reach of a rolling pin, no matter how expertly thrown.